Susie's Corner

A Collection of Inspirational Poems

Alinda C. Daniels

Library of Congress Control Number: 2021915890
ISBN-13:   Paperback: 978-1-64749-631-9

Printed in the United States of America

GoToPublish LLC
1-888-337-1724
www.gotopublish.com
info@gotopublish.com

Contents

Dawn Of A New Day

As I gaze outside my window
At the dawn of a new day.
The greenery puts on a show
And the squirrels are busy at play.

They scamper around the lawn
Searching for food to store.
Along comes Christopher robin
Gathering food as he's done before.

Now a little creature creeps upon this place
Looking for her morning meal.
With hungry eyes upon her face
She spots a treat, a chance she must steal.

It's a beautiful site out my window today
The colors are oh so fine.
Think within my chair I will stay
Until it's time to resign.

A Mothers Love

I'm with you when you're down and out
Or when you've lost your best friend
I'll be there when your heart is broken
Or when the good times end.

I'll never turn my back on you
And I expect the same it's true
Don't take my gifts for granted
It would break my heart into.

I don't expect being perfect
But always do your very best
You'll always be a winner
No matter what the test.

A mother's love is beyond comprehension
No one could ever understand
The depth of her heart for her child
Is always ready to expand.

Love and honor me is my wish
And goodness you'll always release
Be assured that I will rest
When I close my eyes and sleep in peace.

The Journey

I've set out on a journey, don't have a clue where it will lead me. It's exciting and real and oh so new. It's an adventure I've wanted all my life since I was 15 but never pursued it. It's a journey that involves a lot of work and not much travel. So far I've been to some waterfalls and a get-away in the woods and a meadow where children play. Still have a lot of places to go and time to fill. Wanted to start something new so Ii ventured out beyond my computer and touched the hands of someone who wanted to make my journey complete. It was a challenging step to take and I hope I can make it. I set out on my journey on April 25th and still pursuing it. Almost at the end and ready to see the rewards of my journeys. It's a pleasurable journey and met a lot of new friends. Just to let you know - I am having my first book published within the next few weeks. I'm excited!

This won't be my final journey. I have a mansion I want to go to some day!

© Alinda C Daniels, 06/05/2019

Memories All Around

There are memories all around me
In every song I play
In every little moment
I can almost hear you say
Hey, let's take a stroll
Down memory lane together
Doesn't matter the time of day
Nor even the type of weather

Just rest your love on my shoulder
I'll carry you a while
I can feel your tender touch
I can see your gentle smile
I can smell the sweat of your body
As you caress me in your arms
I can feel the strength you exert
When you protect me from all harm

Gosh I wish you were here with me
The days seem awfully long
But then I know just where you are
And I know it's where you belong
But one sweet day I'll be right there
And again we'll be joined side by side
Where death cannot separate us
Where in heaven we'll reside.

True Friends

Met a lot of people in my time.
A lot of different folks I've seen.
Yet there's only a few who are sublime
And those who aren't so very keen.

But only a few can pass the test
Of loyalty, truth and faithfulness
Those to whom are chosen the best
Are those of which I am richly blessed.

To find a true friend to stay by your side
Through good times and bad times, too
It takes some extra work they cannot hide
And it depends on the same from you.

Don't be of you a friend so demanding
Treat them honestly and they will stay.
Be always open and understanding
And they will never leave or stray.

The Burro

The burro is an awkward sight
No beauty he beholds
But listen to this story of the night
As his uniqueness will unfold.

It was a cold and frigid evening
When into a village he arrived
There was no room for them to stay in
So in a stable, he would survive.

But on his back was the virgin Mary
Who was to give birth that night
This time and place was not to vary
As the stars shown ever so bright.

A baby was born in the evening's light
In a manger He laid His head.
The shepherds came led by a star so bright
And the burro stayed near the little shed.

This Child of God would soon grow up
And a teacher for those who were lost
He'd face a crowd so corrupt
And die upon a rugged cross.

You see, this creature called the burro
Brought the Savior in on that day to fulfill
The agonizing crucifixion with much sorrow
Upon the place called Golgatha Hill.

05/05/2019, Alinda C Daniels

Bored To Tears

I'm bored to tears
The little old lady sadly said
Yes bored to tears
Just lying here in this hospital bed.

Nothing to do
And no one to see
No where to go
It's morn and a quarter to three.

The visitors are gone
Not one single peep
And the nursery of little ones
Has finally gone to sleep.

The nurses silently make their
Rounds To make sure all is well
To end this shift without any event
Would make their jobs done swell.

This little lady finally nods to sleep
And hopefully gets some rest
She's peacefully sleeps the night away
Feeling safe with those who are blessed.

If Time Were Reversed

If I could reverse time
When the clock's not ruling me,
I would gather all the time that was mine
And go on a big shopping spree.

Into a big city with fashionable stores
To fill my wants and needs.
Inside the concrete buildings with many floors
I'd have great time indeed!

I'd pick me out a pair of bell-bottom jeans
The ones I haven't seen in years
And find a shirt that's oh so keen
With logo - Blood, Sweat & Tears.

Next a bandana for my head
And sunglasses for the eyes.
Now I'm "jiving" one has said
Sure is good to be alive!

Guess that's a lot of time it seems
Of a time way back when
Free as birds to live you dreams
But this is now and that was then.

Alinda C Daniels, 05/09//2019

I Am He Who Is In Me

Jesus is the example of who I want to be...
A leader and comforter so others in me will see
I'll walk beside you and gently hold your hand
Pick you up when you fall and help you stand.

Be ye there to follow me as I follow Him
I will lead you even when hope looks grim
I will walk in your footprints as He did in mine
Tell you of my home above that's so divine.

Then when you hear me tell of these things
Be loving to others; you'll see the joy it brings
And judge not those that do you wrong
For it's not your place, it does not belong.

But be an imitator of me as I am of Christ
For by His mercy, I was enticed
Follow in my path that I have laid for you
Be close to the Master, He'll be there too.

'Be imitators of me, as I am of Christ.' 1 Corinthians 11: 1

© 11/28/2020, Alinda C Daniels

<u>Happy Father's Day</u>

My father doesn't need a new shirt
Or even a brand new tie
Not even those kind of gifts
That only money can buy.

He doesn't need a bunch of tools
To do a daily chore
He only wants the love I show
And he wants it more and more.

No fancy jewelry does he want
Or a ring to wear upon his finger
No 'Old Spice' shaving cream
From which the scent doth linger.

He doesn't need a winter coat
Not even a new pair of gloves
The only thing He really wants
Is my everlasting faith and love

You see, He's my HEAVENLY FATHER
And unto him I raise mine eyes
He's living with the angels
Where no one ever dies.

HAPPY FATHER'S DAY TO THE
GREATEST FATHER OF ALL!

Secrets

A secret between you and a friend
Is something shared not passed around.
It usually goes unnoticed and generally ends
And is unknown to others without a sound.

But it takes someone special
To tell your secret to
Someone who is honest and loyal
And proves these traits to you.

A person who listens and does not part
To tell the others what you have told
But hold the secrets in their heart
Until you both are grown and old

Secrets we all have shared
Somewhere along the way
And it's a blessing with whom you bared
That secret from yesterday.

The Money Tree

I have a little money tree
It's on display in my room.
It's not what you think you'll see
So, don't be filled with gloom.

The trunk is gold, the branches, too
Their golden leaves do glow.
It's plays a pleasant little tune
Of which you no doubt know.

It's a musical piece bought long ago
By someone very special to me.
It's a money tree worth more than gold
But, in my room is where it will be.

When I see it on my bookcase
I reminisce of time way back when
Money was tight in any case
But love superseded her purchase then.

With unconditional love, It was bought
'Tis more precious as times go on
The love extended when it was sought
The giver of my money tree is now gone.

Foundations

It is said...

The foundation of any marriage
Is really is a combination of things.
Without **LOVE**, there is no meaning
In those golden wedding rings.

But you can't forget the **TRUST**
It's a mighty strong little word
It's made up of only 5 letters
And sometimes goes unheard.

Then there's **HONESTY** in any relationship
Along with **LOYALTY** to make it strong
Without these two main factors
It's doomed and won't last long.

So, I guess then what I am saying...
Is to make it right from the start
Keep all these things so **FAITHFULLY**
And you'll never grow apart.

Tiny Little Footprints

Tiny little footprints, walking in the sand
Walking right beside him, holding mama's hand.
Such a pleasant sight for eyes to see
Walking so playfully - carelessly and free.

Then a swarm of waves quickly rush in
Retaining the level of sand again.
Washing away his presence there
Of tiny feet so fragile and bare.

All along the sandy beach the prints do go
And once again they will show.
When tides go out, they're gone away
But anxiously awaiting another day.

So off again to walk in the sand
And grasp a hold of mama's hand.
Maybe the waves will be good this time
And leave these tiny footprints of mine!

Hollywood Here & Now

You don't have to go to Hollywood
To see all the stars
Just look around you everywhere
And you'll see, where you are - they are.

Actors come in also sort of sizes
Either short, medium or tall
They're usually right beside you
And they can be big or small.

You can always tell just what's in mind
By the words that they speak
Just listen very closely
When 'ere they reach their peak.

It's true most people put up a front
When faced with opposition
But if you'll watch their actions
You'll learn their true position.

You see, Hollywood isn't that far away
It's really at your front door
If you react to one's fantasies
It just encourages them that much more.

So take it from someone who's seen
A glassy-eyed monster within reach
And learn to back off graciously
And with quietness, you'll calm their speech.

The Puppet

It's been a long couple of months of trials and I feel like someone greater than any man alive is pulling the strings of my life and my heart.

It seems that directions are not going the way I had planned and I am beginning to quiver at the decisions being made. But, yet, I know that I must solely rely on the answers I am given.

Prayer has been my constant companion from the anguished feelings. It's a though my left side of my mind if fighting with my right side. The strings of life are getting tighter and tighter and I feel the one controlling the heart is being stretched to it's limit.

I know that what will be, will be for the best but somewhere along the way, feelings and hopes and dreams could be shattered. Then another string will be clipped - the string of love.

It's such a burden to feel pulled in so many directions. But I have faith that the Master of the strings of my life will control them and keep them from becoming a tangled mess.

© 05/26/2019 ,Alinda C Daniels

Don't Speak Ill Of My Christ

I've told you once, I've told you twice
Don't ever speak ill of my Christ
He gave His life for us all
Yes, He answered God's call.

He died upon a rugged cross
People thought He was a total loss
But three days later He arose
Making known His plans disclose.

Promising us all that when we die
We'll join Him in the heavenly sky
If we've accepted His loving plan
If we've place our life in His hand.

The Heavenly Father is always there
To lead and guide, love and care
He'll never slip away from you
He'll make you into someone new.

Just accept the fact that He is real
And His love within you is instilled
Accept His death and resurrection
Seek His guidance and protection.

Loving Memories

Your gentle face and patient smile
With sadness we recall
You had a kindly word for each
And died beloved by all.

Your voice is mute and stilled the heart
That loved us well and true
Ah, bitter was the trial to part
From one so good as you.

You are not forgotten loved one
Nor will you ever be
As long as life and memory last
We will remember thee.

We miss you now, our hearts are sore
As times goes by, we miss you more
Your loving smile, your gentle face
No one can fill your vacant place.

Originally written 07/23/1982 in honor of our Dad...on this day God took
an angel home. It's been 39 years but it seems like yesterday.

© 07/12/2021, Alinda C Daniels

Two Peas In A Pod

If I were one of two peas in a pod
I would want the other to be Job, servant of God.
A man of great patience and faith so strong
I know he would never let me do wrong.
He would suffer and pay a great price
But never would he let me make a sacrifice.
He'd tell me to stand up to the test
Don't give in to Satan - he's not the best.
"Just do what is right," he would say to me,
"My pea in my pod, Eternity you will see!"
My strength and my life I owe to him
Following his footsteps has been a great gem.

<u>The Coming Home Party</u>

It's a party for someone special who left too soon
Before the Forget Me Nots had just started to bloom
We gathered to say goodbye, then retreated to our home
And left him in this garden place all alone.

But then around midnight, I awoke in a tremble
Sounded like Heaven was adding her own rumble.
Thunder was laughing in an unusual way
It wasn't too far but close by it did stay

It almost seemed like a joyous celebration
To welcome someone home after a long vacation.
I thought to myself, my dad is home
He's waited for this party much to long!

It continued into the late of night
It seemed so joyful in Heaven so bright.
The gifts he receives will never end
And now he has a Father on who he can depend.
Welcome Home Dad!

Only Time Will Tell

It was not the average conversation
To be held behind the closed door
Just to believe these were His creation
Made me wonder what was in store.

I figured only time will tell
When one of them would stop the fuss
But neither one would say they failed
So it seemed their words were still a must.

They finally reached a meeting of minds
And out the door they went
Didn't think of what they left behind
And the time they lost was gone and spent.

Love is precious so listen to what you say
Over silly, meaningless insinuations
When one could be easily be taken away
In the blink of an eye in any situation.

A Dream???

As I walked down the dusty road
I came upon an lonely old toad.
He greeted me with a witty smile
And ask if he could walk with me awhile?

To look at him just seemed grotesque
But being a loner, too, I told him yes.
We laughed and talked for such a long while
Must have been at least a mile.

The more I talked, the more he knew
The more he could later review.
You'll have much pleasure to get to know
But the right choice you must show.

Then the road parted left and right
And it was beginning to get night.
He ask me if I could grant him one wish
I ask him what...he said a kiss!

I said a kiss! You must be crazy
Then my world seemed so hazy.
All of a sudden I sat up with a scream
I had awaken so abruptly from a dream!

God Never...

My God is real. He never sleeps
And I know He's here with me
From sunrise mornings when days just begin
Until the sunset marks the day's end.

Whenever sleepless nights awaken me
Right beside me is where He'll always be.
We sit and talk about problems of the day
He reassures me they, too, will go away.

When fright creeps deep inside
He'll never run away and hide.
I feel His warm and tender embrace
And gentle hands as He strokes my face.

At times, tears of loneliness are unable to bare
But God listens and shows me He really cares.
He dries my eyes, plants a kiss on my head
Then in just a few minutes, I'm back in bed.

God will never leave you, nor forsake you
In any time of pain or need - it's true
Just reach out your hands, you'll see
Call upon Him, He's just waiting for thee!

© 06/10/2019, Alinda C Daniels

<u>In The Midst of Trouble</u>

Sometimes things get into turmoil
And I know not which way to turn
The moments seem to happen so fast
That my life begins to churn.

I reach out for some support
But I can't explain my mess
But I know that God is listening
So to him I must confess.

I will not fear nor sustain to worry
When I feel the bad times come
For I know that God is with me
And He will protect me from the storm.

God be with me and those I love
Protect us from dangers that may come
Keep all of us away from evil
And deliver us safely to our homes.

Though I walk in the midst of trouble, thou wilt revive me: Thou shalt stretch forth thine hand against the wrath of mine enemies, and thy right hand shall save me. Psalm 138:7

© 06/20/2021, Alinda C Daniels

In The Blink Of An Eye

If I could go back in time,
Sixteen is where I'd choose.
It was a time when life was fun
And you didn't worry about the news.

I had a "Sweet 16" party
Given by my aunt and mom.
Yes, even the boys were there,
That's why there were chaperons!

At school, pep rallies for our football team
On a special Friday night game were keen.
With half-time bands in full harmony
And the crowning of our homecoming queen.

Things went great and school days were fun
And the snacks just have to be mentioned.
RC Colas & Moon Pies; Soda pops & salty nuts
But this particular year, the principal got our full attention.

Continued next page

Everyone got deathly quiet as he told the news
"President John F Kennedy has been shot."
Times look grave for the family and nation,
I think we all were in a state of shock.

Schools let out the next couple of days
And most everyone watched and shared.
The horse signifying no rider, the eternal flame
All carried out and the service ended in prayer.

But to top it all was a little boy's salute
To say goodbye to his loving dad.
Just signified how times can change
In the blink of an eye from good to bad.

I learned that year not to take life for granted,
It can be just a matter of time.
When God puts His plan in motion
And The Creator makes up His mind.

© 07/21/2019, Alinda C Daniels

Present, Past, Future

You get up in the morning, grab your coffee and the news
Sip on your java and fuss about how the world is treating you.
It's all about walls, abortions, riots and strikes
The world's in a mess - that's in very plain site.

Politicians sit on Capitol Hill and it seems I must confess
That no one wants to agree to end this ugly mess
It's meetings after meetings until time to adjourn
And again they'll meet another day to take another turn.

I know they have a job to do but what is it I ask?
To dwell on something that happened in the past?
So far Old Dixie has been released from her place of existence
And the monuments are right behind her without any resistance.

Our Pledge of Allegiance, our money too,
Wants to remove God's name - it's true.
The 10 Commandments and The Bible are wanted out of school
That's so unfair - just seems so unjustly cruel!

Next, we might be forced to take down the Red, White and Blue.
Then what will AMERICA do ?
Fall to our knees asking God for help?
He might just answer "I've got nothing left."

American Made

It's good to be an American
Where Old Glory waves her colors proudly
Where freedom is so very real
And everyone accepted most gladly.

Where Lady Liberty stands tall and strong
Holding on without mistakes
She greets the poor, the tired and weary
Who enter through her gates.

To those who cannot understand
The freedom that we share
There is no other place than the USA
That one can even compare.

So hands up to the Red, White and Blue
With fireworks and sparklers at night
And to Lady Liberty standing alone
May her torch forever burn bright.

The Rose of Sharon & Christ

Have you ever noticed The Rose of Sharon
And depicted the perfection of each flower?
The petals are perfectly set in place
A strong plant that has stamina and power.

The white flower indicates Christ's purity
As the purple signifies the royalty He bears.
The red signifies the blood He shed
And the center stem is the crown He wears.

The Rose of Sharon shows life lines
Just as we must be the followers
There is no greater love than the love of Christ
Nor none more perfect than this gifted flower.

To compare this flower to Jesus Christ
With all the love we know
Could only mean the more it is watered
The more love He will forever show.

© 06/17/2019, Alinda C Daniels

<u>A Stranger I Met</u>

It was my first day out alone
And I spent it just driving around
Rode up toward the Blue Ridge Mountains
And think I covered every town.

Stopped by the Time Drive Inn
And ordered myself a plate
Didn't know how long I'd be out
Didn't want to stay away too late.

Nearing home I turned down a road
And I heard a muffled shout
And experienced a quick jerk to the right
Oh my gosh, I've had a blowout.

Alone on the roadside I began to panic
Never changed a tire in my life
Looked at the flattened mess
Became skeptical, full of strife.

Didn't have a cellphone to call home
They hadn't been invented yet
Then a stranger just happened by
Someone whom I had never met.

Continued next page

Daddy always said be careful of strangers
And this man was a stranger to me
But took a chance when he looked at the flat
And said he could fix it for free.

So he wrestled with the tightened lugs
And one lug slipped and cut his cheek
It looked so awful, such a mess
But he was so quiet, didn't even speak.

I wondered would he be angry at me
For his stopping by to help me out
But today I learned a lesson in life
What a good Samaritan is all about.

I was grateful to this man
Who befriended me that day
And I sure was very thankful
That he's the one who came my way.

<u>Silent Whispers</u>

As I walked from room to room
I breathe the breath of choice
Like sweet magnolias beginning to bloom
I suddenly felt the whispers of your voice.

It was as though you said, "Hello"
But as I turned, you weren't there.
I ask myself where did you go?
Your voice I hear, but, of you I am unaware.

And, just as quietly you said, "Wait"
Eagerly, I looked your way again
Still all I could see was empty space
I wonder why did this all begin?

It was words he didn't have time to say
Last whispers of words still due
"Until we meet again some sweet day"
Silent whispers saying, "I Love You, too!"

Faded Memories - Alzheimer's

Today the sunshine rests upon my face
And the good Lord above shows me His grace.
I'm still the same as sure as I can be
But something is different I cannot see.

My family is with me, I know them not
Oh my, it seems that I forgot.
Their names are on the tip of my tongue
But my days go back to when they were young.

The memories are fading though they seem
To be captured in a distant dream.
My constant thoughts seem engraved in stone
Makes me wonder what's going on.

I think I'm losing my mind no doubt
I don't understand what it is all about.
Just forgetfulness from growing old???
No, it's more than that, I'm told.

Memories get worse has the days go by
Some days I feel alone, but don't know why.
These feelings leave me frightened you see
As my mind can't remember this person inside of me.

Tribute to my mom who passed away with Alzheimer's. God bless all those who have connections to anyone with this disease. Just be patient and understand their present situation and love them as a little child - Enjoy them.

© 07/23/2019, Alinda Daniels

First Steps

When we are born we cannot walk
But then as we grow we are taught.
First steps are always hardest to take
We are feeble and our legs always shake.

Without the help from a loving hand
We would surely fall when we stand.
Much is the same when accepting our Savior
We learn to walk and gain his favor.

We seek the hand of someone we trust
We step with confidence this is a must
To feel the Almighty's gentle caress
Will lead us into everlasting happiness.

Just as we reach for that trustworthy hand
We seek the strength to rise and stand
We take our first steps every day
Knowing that God will lead the way.

So when you walk with God by your side
Hold your head up high with pride
Remember your steps on that first day
And know he'll be beside you all the way.

I Will Succeed

If love was forever, I'd never blue
I'd never be lonely, I'd never miss you.
I'd never question where you had gone
Or why I was left all alone

But time has a way to challenge a love
It's all in the hands of the Man above.
It's a day by day lifetime endeavor
Some to last forever and ever.

But you, my love, came along in life
And erased all my toils and strife.
I found not only love but a friend
Who stayed beside me until the end.

Once again life throws me a curve
And the future is another big blur.
But I will rise up to succeed
And be the winner God wanted me to be.

I Can Only Imagine

I can only imagine a world without fear,
the constant happiness without a tear
or maybe laugher that never ends,
and even the warmth a soft word sends.

A tranquil solace of blissful peace
when troubles and trials finally cease.
To know the feeling of relaxation
goes beyond my scope of imagination.

The life I have sought for so long
once I face the great unknown.
What a tremendous joy behold
when I walk those streets of gold.

To face the Master of the plan
and He takes me by the hand.
"Welcome home my child," he'll say.
Oh what a glorious, blessed day!

Hello World

Hello world,
can't you stopped a while?
Spinning out of control
is really not my style.

Need to slow it down
and catch a breath or two.
Catch up on news in town
and find out who is who.

Take the time to recall
the memories of the past.
Remember tales of the fall
and a love that forever lasts.

It's the little moments you neglect
that really cost you time.
To go back to a point select,
will make you lose your mind.

So slow down world, take time to play
you're going way to fast.
Catch me up to yesterday
and make life worth a blast!

<u>G I Joe</u>

"G I Joe" is the toy size man
Of whom all the children become a fan
He's a unique soldier, truly one of a kind
That comes to every child's mind.

But my "G I Joe" was a real life soldier
Who was stronger and a lot bolder
Crossing the lines when he knew best
Always meant he was put to the test.

He fought the war that was far away
And came back home to stay
But the battles he had in his life
Caused him much pain and strife.

Reminders of the war he fought
Left him weak and distraught
These were battles of memories
That he recalled took place in history.

His mind played over the battle afar
That left so many wounds and scars
Chills and sweats he had at night
Dreaming of being filled with fright.

Now he's resting in eternal peace
Where all the pain and fears cease
No more tears and dreams of war
He's in God's loving arms for ever more.

© 04/01/2021, Alinda C Daniels

Magical Moment

Poem Prompt:
If I Could Fly
by Jonathan Potter

If I could fly
My plane to you
I'd put the sky
Into my shoe
And make my way
Across the blue
In half a day
That's what I'd do
To spend the evening
Touching you
And then the morning
Through and through
And on and on
And deep into
Your dusk my dawn
Our one from two

Follow Up Poem"
Magical Moments
By Alinda Daniels

Oh how happy we would be
When I see you and you see me
Tender hugs we would share
Oh, just to know you really care
Sharing a love that is true
Total happiness for me and you
Don't let this magical moment end
All I have to you I send
And when our time is finally 'ore
And we separate once more
I'll travel again across the blue
Putting the sky in my shoe

© 04/24/2021, Alinda C Daniels

<u>Beyond The Gate</u>

In the garden stands an old gate
Covered with weeds and vines
But just inside the inner break
Lived a life so very fine.

The gentleman of the house, they say
Was one of eccentric taste
One to never throw away
Nor one to ever make a waste.

He lived such a life of leisure
That the house had sagging walls
The upkeep was not his pleasure
And the walls began to fall.

You see, the value of what he owned
Was truly not his concern
So he had to leave his cozy home
And a dreadful lesson he did learn.

Take care of your possessions
And give them attention due
Don't hoard earthly obsessions
They'll get the best of you.

Lost In Your Arms Tonight

I've planned all day for our special date
Getting so excited, can hardly wait
Gonna go out and dine and dance
To some music of love and romance.

Then we'll walk on our nightly stroll
While we listen to the ocean waves roll
Holding on tight to a dream come true
Warm caressing arms only from you.

Soon the romance will end tonight
While we hold each other tight
When the moon glistens on the ocean floor
We'll say good night and plan for more.

A goodnight kiss to seal the night
A caressing hug when he holds me tight
Finally goodnight is so hard to say
Sending all my love your way.

Another day and date to plan
Favorite rendezvous with a special man
Feelings of excitement stir deep inside
Where my love for him resides.

Remember When

REMEMBER WHEN...

Close your eyes and go back. Before the Internet or the Mac,
Before semi-automatics and crack, Before chronic and Endo,
before Sega and Nintendo.

WAY BACK...
I'm talking about - Hide and go seek at dusk, Sitting on the
porch, hot bread and butter. Eatin' a super, dooper sandwich,
red light – green light, chocolate milk, lunch tickets. Penny
candy in a brown paper bag, hopscotch, butterscotch.
Double Dutch, Jacks, kickball, dodgeball, Y'all! Mother, may
I? Hula hoops and sunflower seeds, jaw breakers, blow
pops, Mary Janes. Running through the sprinklers (I can't get
wet... All right! Well don't wet my hair!) The smell of the sun
and lickin' salty lips.

WAIT...
Catching lightning bugs in a jar, playing with a sling shot and
playing Red Rover. When around the corner seemed so far
away and going "downtown" seemed like going somewhere.
Bedtime prayers, climbing trees and a million mosquito bites
and scraping our knees! Sticky fingers, Cops and Robbers,
Cowboys and Indians. Sitting on the curb, jumping down
the step. Jumping in the bed, full of energy and pep. Pillow
fights, being tickled to death, running and playing 'til you
were out of breath! Laughing so hard that your stomach hurt,
being tired from all the playing... Remember that???

NOW, can you remember when...
There were two types of sneakers for girls and boys – Keds
and Flyers. And the only time you wore them were at gym.
Dime Stores and soda pops, ice cream sodas and
sweets. When nearly everyone's mom was there when kids
got home from

school. When nobody owned a purebred pet, when a quarter was a descent allowance and another quarter... A huge bonus! When you reached into a muddy gutter to get a penny. When girls never dated nor kissed until late high school, when your mom wore nylons that came in two pieces. When all your male teachers wore neckties and female teachers had their hair done weekly. When you got your car windshield cleaned and gas pumped without asking and free every time. And you didn't pay for air and you got trading stamps too boot!

WHEN...

Laundry detergent had free glasses, dishes or towels hidden inside the box. When parents could discipline their kids or feed them milk and cornbread or ask them to help with the groceries and nobody, not even the kids, thought a thing of it. When it was considered a privilege to be taken out to dinner with parents at a real restaurant. When they kept kids back a grade if they failed... And did! When being sent to principal's office was nothing compared to the fate that awaited a misbehaving student at home....
Basically, we were in fear of our lives but wasn't because of drive by shootings, drugs or gangs but disapproval from our parents and grandparents was a much bigger threat!

I AIN'T FINISHED, YET...

What about the girl who had the bubbly handwriting! Licking the beaters when mom made a cake. Doesn't it feel good to go back and say, "YEAH, I remember that!" There's nothing like the good old days. They were good then and good now when we think about them. Share some of these thoughts with someone you love. One can't be serious all the time!

Random thought of years ago.

© 04/--/2019, Alinda C Daniels

<u>Depression</u>

As I sit here and listen to the world outside,
all I feel is emptiness deep inside.

I try to hide this pain within my mind
as I fumble through the day
but nothing eases the thoughts unkind
they just won't go away!

Alas some tears have shown their way
to help to ease this dreadful pain
if only for a little part of the day
I can from these feelings refrain.

And now the night is falling
as sleepiness begins to come.
My sanctuary is gently calling
Come home weary one - come home.

The Nap

Have you ever wondered how it would be to go to sleep when something went horribly wrong and then wake up just in the nick time, when everything and everyone was talking together and laughing and seemingly having a good and peaceful time lasting forever?

Yep that's how it was when I was growing up.
I'd go to sleep when things got rough, I slept through the bad times turning on like an alarm clock and going off when the danger was over. It's strange to look back on the way my mind protected me without me understanding or doing it unknowingly.

Now I long for that time way back then when I could sleep my problems and dangers away but it doesn't come quite so easily. There's too much bitterness or unhappiness in the world it seems - no one can escape this terrible environment that we live in today.

Oh for a nap!

The Rain

Watch the clouds come rolling in
Hear the patter of the rain
Time to steal a moment's simplicity
Of which nature can't refrain.

Listen to the raindrops
dancing upon the roof.
Caring not which way they fall
Eagerly aloof.

Feel the cleanliness in the air
Smell the freshness anew
Watch the happy raindrops
Bring out the child in you.

Jump in all the puddles
Splashing to and fro
Listen, mom is calling
Time for us to go.

The 'Tea' Party

"Let's have a tea party," said the little girl of ten
Just a few neighbors and my closest friends.
I'll have in the kitchen near the patio deck
Hope it's not raining - oh what the heck!

I'll use the special tea set Santa gave to me
The one with flowers and cute bumble bees
I'll ask Ann and Andy to join the party fun
And Ken and Barbie - the list is almost done.

Oh, don't forget to ask Babe and Barny bears
Gonna be great to see everybody there!
I'll serve Oreo cookies to the honored guests
And white milk...well, it's got to be the best.

It's going to be so fun, just you wait and see.
I'll wear my new dress mama bought for me.
Guess I'm through planning my special event
Think I'll go and play, the day is almost spent.

A House...A Home

You can build yourself a big, fancy house
filled with nails and two-by-fours
a roof to keep the rains out
and beautiful wooden floors.

You can add a sofa and a chair
and a kitchen to keep family fed
then some pictures covering up walls so bare
now, a big oak bed to rest your weary head.

You can add a family - a mom and a dad
and children to fill each room.
But, without the love it would be so sad
This house would surely end in doom.

So, fill your house with lots of love
and see what it becomes.
Count your blessings from above
You'll see your house becomes your Home.

Abigail

While walking in the hall of work one day
I saw a tractor with a web out a window bay
The author was working in the morning dew
As she wove the web so beautiful and new.

So, I took a picture of the web and the tractor
As pretty as it was, that wasn't the main factor.
You see, I had caught a glimpse of something so bright
That left an outline of heavenly light.

I thought when I saw it, it was an odd sight
But I had captured my angel taking flight.
Nothing around to make that reflection
No overcast of clouds to my recollection.

Her graceful wings spread out to show
Her flight from here she must go.
A stream of light pushing her up and away
I had met my guardian angel, Abigail, that day.

Home Where The Heart Is

A home is where you lay your head
When you go to sleep at night.
You feel safe and warm within your bed
Away from fear and fright.

But in this universe so big outside
Wherever you may roam
You can venture far and wide
But always look forward to coming home.

Whenever you travel and a new place you face
You'll find everything is as you need.
Make the most of His giving grace
Cause satisfaction is guaranteed.

So, no matter where you're apt to go
Be grateful to have a home so bliss
Rest assure that you will know.
That the heart is where the home is.

Ask, Seek, Knock

ASK and it shall be given unto you
But only if you believe
The Lord has promised - it is true
But His acceptance you must receive.

SEEK and you shall find the answer
The wisdom that you need
To know Him and only Him do you serve
Your heart and soul, He'll feed.

Answer the **KNOCK** - He patiently awaits
But to ignore it, He'll walk away
Don't ignore this meeting date
There may not be another day.

<u>God Is In Control</u>

God is in control
Of this I know is true
It only takes believing
And it takes that of you.

You must have faith to be on top
When troubles come your way.
Stand strong in beliefs, do no stop
Do not linger and do not sway.

If you stumble, if you fall
Or get lost along the way
Just listen to your heart's call
And you'll surely never sway.

Trust with all your heart and soul
And things will surely change
Seek highly your wishes and your goal
And within God's plan, He will arrange.

The Toucan

There once was a toucan
Which was a nosey bird
He belong to this senior man
Who was equally absurd.

When ask to "birdsit" one fine day
I said yes with some hesitation;
If only he'll be in his cage
When I arrived at my destination.

Upon arrival I met Toucan Mounty
And feathers flew everywhere.
He became my special bounty
But would be forced to leave him there.

He kept saying, "Pretty bird, hungry bird."
Without ever moving his large beak.
Becoming quite a persistent little nerd
All too able to explicitly speak.

Just one more hour to be his sitter
And I'll be on going on my way
Oh the thought of being a non-quitter
Would make it a pleasant, quiet day!

The Portrait

Time to get a family portrait
To send to mom and dad
Couldn't keep the children straight
The photographer was getting mad.

Susie would not stop giggling
Tommy kept pulling at his tie
Johnny couldn't stop wiggling
And big Bill was ready for goodbye.

Still determined to get it done
I offered them a treat.
The victory I had finally won
And all were nice and neat.

The portrait was a great success
But not without work indeed.
It is done - now for the rest
Now off to get some Mickey D's!

Daddy Was The Best

Daddy was the best a girl could ever want
His was a soft spoken, gentle man
Easy going man, very nonchalant
But always willing to take a stand.

His demeanor was that of a upright guy
He never raised his temper high
And never gave up or quit.
He was someone you couldn't forget.

He stood up for what he believed in
He served his country with pride
He fought for freedom but in the end
He suffered with great stride.

He always said he was living on borrow time
He had escaped death's fatal blow
When the enemy delivered the gruesome crime
And his sister ship at sea was set aglow.

Seeing him tell this story so true
Would bring whelps of tears to his eyes
He couldn't escape the sounds that blew
And the clouds of smoke that filled the skies.

You see, among other things, he was my hero
A treasure and my friend
He had longed for that peaceful place to go
When borrowed time had reached it's end.

<u>Proud Peacock</u>

Peacocks are a most exotic creature
Their beauty is beyond compare
Just vision their unique feature
As they spread their feathers into the air.

The peacock's tail has hundreds of "eyes"
That represent protection and immorality.
They wear them with much glamour and pride
As they absorb the vibes of negativity.

Their reputation as a friendly bird
Is not necessarily known of this gem.
They can be rather rude and absurd
When food is dangled in front of them.

These elegant birds are a sight to see
Prancing on land or flying in the air.
It's such as wonderous place to be
Among the peacock, you need to be there.

My Poet's Corner

It's takes a good day for rhymes to be
Within my thoughts so fresh and free.
No one to chase my thoughts away
Yep, that makes for a well spent day.

Quiet moments have come and went
Especially in my typical events.
Suddenly a quiet thought slips in
And quickly I reach for my favorite pen.

Jotting the words down on a writing pad
Determining later if it is good or bad.
Reading over the poem, I begin to edit
Giving way to some, others getting credit.

Now the thoughts are filling my mind
So much to do and so many rhymes.
A slack moment don't seem to find
Just give me a minute, just give me some time.

Time to lay down my pen and rest
Guess I've passed my daily test.
Off to bed, I'm on my way
Tomorrow is another day.

<u>My Gain In Christ</u>

My gain in Christ is never a loss
He keeps me safe from harm
I could never turn on that old rugged cross
Where He stretched out his loving arms.

I've had the loss of earthly treasures
And often become deprived and down
But none can compare to the measure
Of my heavenly home and crown.

You see, without faith there's no tomorrow
Without tomorrow, there is no hope
And without these I'd have much sorrow
Without Christ's love, I simply couldn't cope.

He is my reason for living each day
With Christ I will never roam
His love for me never goes away
And some day He'll take me home.

God love the One who came to earth
To save me from my sins
I cry each time I see His sacrifice
And I know this was not the end.

God Gets The Credit

Did you wake up this morning
To a wonderful, blissful day
Give God the credit
He saw it in His plan today.

Did you notice the singing birds
As they flew within your sight
And did you hear the squirrels
As they nest food for the night.

Did you notice the tall, tall trees
And the flowers as they bloom
How about the signs of nature
As they scatter to find their room.

Did you notice the sky above
Was it blue or a tint of grey
Could mean the sun will shine
Or you'll have can rainy day.

Just think of the wonderful things
That God has given you
It's time to thank Him for the gifts
And give Him the credit that is due.

Traditions Throughout The Year

Fads usually come then go away
But traditions are here to stay
Here's a few to mention for you own rendition
Some can be added a welcome addition.

In January a New Year's Eve party to celebrate
A new calendar this Day will make.
A February Valentine card for a special sweetheart
And March's St Patty's Day pinch is just a start.

The April Easter Story if customarily told
Or Easter egg hunt with colors so bold.
Then don't forget mom on May's Mother's Day
On June's Father's Day give dad his say.

Celebrate Independence Day on 4th of July
Beware of August's first day of schoolwhen kids ask, "Why?
Rest your weary bones in September when Labor Day is seen
And carve a pumpkin in October for Halloween.

Say your prayers over a November Thanksgiving meal
Leaving Christ out of Christmas in December just isn't real.
Share these traditions with those you love
Being sure to thank the good Lord above.

The Loss Of A Great Man

Many men were not as great
As the President of the United States.
He has to worry about his land
And always be able to take his stand.

Presidents living and some yet gone
Must stand up to his rights as a building of stone.
Taking his hardships both present and past
The President must complete his hardships and tasks.

Many of America's men must face many dangers
As they face much hatred and anger
Hatred can only be ample
To give this story as an example.

They must face a chance of assassination
As they make their debut to the entire nation.
And this is one story of a great loss
When America failed to keep her boss.

It began in Dallas on a clear, windy day
As President Kennedy came here to stay.
All at once came a ringing, an unheard of knock
And our President had undoubtedly been shot.

Continued next page

Drooping over on the lap of his wife
Everyone was praying, "Dear God, give him life."
Rushing and racing to the hospital in fear
The death of our President was soon drawing near.

Waiting and hoping and working in vain
Our late President was released from his pain.
Sadness had come to our nation at last
And the red, white, and blue was lowered half-mast.

People were crying and soldiers were blue
And the funeral escorts were part of his crew.
Marching reverently as they carried this man
Everyone knew he was in great hands.

Over the bridge to the place of his rest
God be with his family and may they always be blessed.

Alinda Crenshaw (Daniels)
63 - '64 school year

The Wall

The Vietnam Veterans Memorial
Stands proud in Washington, D C
It's names upon the polished granite walls
Are there for all to see.

Dedicated on Veterans Day of 1982,
It tells a story so tragic and so true
The walls contain more than 58, 000 names
From soldiers to four nurses, too.

It's made up of two long black granite slabs
With 72 separate panels to make up each wall
The names are etched in the order of death
And MIAs, POW's are included in it all.

So many soldiers suffered a loss
So many didn't come home
It was a war so gallantly fought
So many fought bewildered and alone.

Yet, some were reported missing
Maybe even prisoners of war
But still there was the draft
Because Uncle Sam wanted more.

The names begin and end at the center
Where they join and are meant to form a circle
To indicate the ending to the war
And to survive was the greatest miracle.

It's worth the time to see this solemn site
And reflect when walking the path
'Tis a tribute to those named here
"No greater love doth a soldier hath..."

The Midnight Hungries

I went to bed kinda early
Without my typical munchies
Tossed and turned, finally fell asleep
And entered a dream of crunchies.

I saw a red, furry creature
Who looked hungry as could be
Then a ghostly little guy
Who scared the life out of me!

At the table was an olger
Who was ruler of this shack
He told us all to take heed
There will be "No more midnight snacks."

All at once I sat upright in my bed
And at the clock I really stared
I was shaking from lack of crunchies...
I had had a midnight nightmare!

So off to the kitchen I did go
To clear my clouded mind
I'll get me a midnight snack
To myself, I will be kind.

The Time To Pray

The time to pray is now
For a nation whose gone astray
We'll raise our tight gripped hands
And ask God to show the way.

But it will take a nation
Praying earnestly and sincere
To make a change in worldly events
And trust change will soon be here.

So let's all pray for guidance
With clasped hands to God above
Pray for peace and order
Filled with the Almighty's love.

"To clasp the hands in prayer is the beginning of an uprising against the disorder of the world ". Karl Barth

© 08/03/2019, Alinda C Daniels

Always On Camera

You're always on camera
So be your very best
You're always in the movies
So be alert and pass the test.

He always has you in His view
So stay clear and always in focus
Don't let the light dim on you
Don't change your true locus.

Rest assure you're being recorded
Of every word and breath you take
Just remember who's holding the camera
And He records your every mistake.

Be sure of your screenplay
It portrays the true you
It always records every decision you make
And every avenue that you choose.

Yes, your life is a living movie
And you're the leading star
You're captured twenty-four-seven
So be careful who you are.

Love Is A Gift

Nothing can express my love for you,
Not even words of deepest meaning
Only feelings that are very true
Can leave a scar or inside a tingling.

It is a feeling of great happiness and joy
And is always, always sent.
It is expressed by the right girl or boy
And true love is always present.

Ye both hold each other closely
As you discuss your future thrills
Then you tell everyone boastfully
And your heart is filled with chills.

Oh yes, the expression of love fills each lover's soul
And is the greatest yet to come
A true love expression is the best to be told
And the best to happen to some.

Alinda Crenshaw (Daniels), 06/23/1966

The Tribute

I attended a most unusual funeral today
Which really seemed so grand
It was for a veteran of a battle
That took place in a foreign land.

The escorts marched in cadence
As they brought the soldier to rest
A new American flag
Was draped across the coffin crest.

The Reverend had some touching words
An eulogy, a tribute, and a prayer
Then unknowingly a twenty-one gun salute
Was shot into the air.

It was such a tearful service
I just froze with hands in my lap
But oh the tears did fall
When in a distance, a bugler played "Taps."

The Hammock

I bought myself a hammock
It looked so neat on TV
It was one of those for the outdoors
That hung between two trees.

Well I finally got it hung in place
Could hardly wait to take the test
To see if it would hold me up
So I could get some rest.

Went inside to grab a blanket
And a pillow for my head
This would definitely be a challenge
Climbing into this swinging bed.

Well, one leg into the hammock
Oh gosh I'm doing fine
Gotta get my body next
To the center line.

Finally got the whole of me
Into the swaying hole
Tried to turn my body over
Oh boy, it began to roll!

This experience is not worth the pain
Of going round and round
Guess I'll choose my queen size bed
It's better than the ground.

Old Fashion Love

I met him on a blind date
Was nervous as could be
Just waiting for his arrival
Wishing him I could see.

My mind were running freely
My heart was racing fast
My legs felt weak as spaghetti
He's here, he's here at last!

He was a quiet kind of guy
With salt and pepper hair
A simple minded six foot giant
Not pushy or putting on an "air."

Continued next page

He approached me very shyly
And slowly touched my hand
I knew right from that moment
That he was a special man.

He took his time at courting
He became my very best friend
You see he became the love of my life
He was definitely my God send.

Dedicated to the man I love whom God took home in July 2012. I love you Joe!

© 08/03/2019, Alinda C Daniels

<u>Getting Old</u>

I'm not a happy camper
Today is not my day
It seems like everyone
Has gone their separate way.

It's just that I'm feeling the loneliness
And no one to tell it to
Makes quite a difference when it's silent
Makes me somewhat blue.

Use to have my little ones
To make up all the noise.
But they're all grown up now
And have their own little set of joys.

This is just another stage in life
The age of growing old
To face unpredictable bouts of silence
As I live in my Days of Gold.

The Bible Tells Me So

The Bible has sixty-six books in the edition
And has many stories and truths within
It tells of the earth's glorious creation
But tells of how God will bring it to an end.

It's thousands of years old you must be aware
And it's always on the best seller list
It speaks of a Garden beyond compare
And how God is always in the mist.

It tells you of a miraculous birth
When Mary was just a virgin girl
It speaks of wise men and shepherds
Who traveled all over the world.

It takes you up to Calvary's hill
On the day Mary's son, Jesus, died
The thorny crown, the driven nails
My God, my God...He cried.

Then at last in three days He arose
And the reign of our Savior began
He'll gather His children some sweet day
When the Father comes back again.

<u>Hello God It's Me Again</u>

While sitting in a frantic cue
I ask God what I'm suppose to do
God, I know not which way to turn
As my stomach begins to churn.

I just keep praying for an answer
Will He send me a sign or enhancer
To meet this heavy internal plea
To mine own heart from Thee.

I trust in Him in every way
Knowing the answer will come I pray
I just have to believe for the best
And wait for Him to complete this request.

Patience is a virtue so I've been told
From early in life til you're very old
Waiting for the answer is truly the way
Turn it over to God, He'll not sway.

You see, when I get overly anxious
I can become very cantankerous
And nothing seems to go my way
And I'm headed for a long, long day.

So, when I reach out to you dear God
To guide me safely wherever I trod
And listen for me as I cry out when
Hello, God, it's me again!

God's Special Little Miracle

Melody was my first born child
A beautiful baby no doubt
At 6 months, stricken with juvenile diabetes
And her world was flipped inside out.

She struggled through her daily life
For many, many years
She had good days and bad days
With lots of laughter and lots of tears.

This disease worked hard on her body
A pancreas and kidney she needed
We took her to the finest doctors
And listened to the words they heeded.

Signed her up on a donor's list
And began a long anticipated wait
Prayed even harder and more fervently
To get her foot through the gate.

Called the doctors the next week on Wednesday
For reassurance she was on the list
Got the news on Friday of same week
My heart raced and my eyes began to mist.

Took her immediately to the distant hospital
God had answered prayers in a prompt way!
She had a pancreas and kidney transplants
The very next day!

Praise God for answered prayers!

<u>Mary Had A Little Lamb</u>

Mary had a little Lamb
Who was born on Christmas day
He was sent here by his Father
To take our sins away.

Because of much grave dislike
This child became a hunted man
He spread good news of everlasting love
Across every nation and every land.

He traveled over land and sea
Spreading His love for all men
He never turned on anyone
Not even at the end.

When Judas gave the kiss of death
To this humble servant
Then he dismissed himself
While the soldiers were being observant.

This Lamb was found guilty
As the crowds cried and cried
Out of the mouths of many
They shouted, "Crucify, Crucify!"

Upon Golgotha Hill and on a rugged cross
This precious Lamb of God was nailed
But in the end of it all
Life over death had prevailed.

He Arose, praise God Almighty,
Jesus Christ is Alive!
And for my hope of eternal
life I surely will strive.

Momma

It's been fourteen long years
Since you were taken away
But in my heart it seems
You've been gone since yesterday.

I can feel your love and tenderness
And the way you dealt with pain
I can feel anxiety when we talked
Gosh, how I wish you were here again.

I remember our first girl talk
And, oh, the advice you gave
Made me shiver in my shoes
Made grandma roll over in her grave.

Now when my date "time" was over
You'd flicker that porch light
On and off it was time
To tell my date goodnight!

You've been through trying times
You've conquered all your fears
You've shared a lot of laughter
And, yes, a lot of tears.

We've sat around the table
You played your guitar and we'd sing
Surrounded by those gospel tunes
We could hear the church bells ring.

Like I said, Momma, it's been fourteen years
And I miss you more each day
But thanks to God above
I would not have had it any other way!
I Love You Momma

<u>God There's You</u>

Sometimes when I'm feeling down
Or even feeling blue
I turn my head around
And look up - God there's you!

You're there in the sunshine
That brings a smile to my face
You're there in my daddy's words
When he bows at supper and says grace.

You're there when I'm playing
And I fall and skin my knee
I shout to you for mercy
And you give it and agree.

You're there at my bedtime
When I'm on my knees in prayer
And I can feel you in my presence
Yes, God, you're always there.

Carry me through the night dear God
And bless me and my buddies, too
Let tomorrow's sun shine in my their faces
So they can smile and say, "God there's you!"

Strictly from a child's view! Each child should feel God's presence no matter where they turn.

Butterfly Marvels

Dainty wings so thin and frail
Small in size but fit to scale.
Flies so delicately with all its power
Searching for the perfect flower.

Beautiful colors make up their wings
With tiny scales that only God brings
They scout out the flowers for nectar
And feed the other flower sectors.

To some they symbolize joy and rebirth
And they are truly known for all their worth
They usually live for short months of twelve
Then give in to nature where they dwell.

So next time you see a butterfly in flight
Remember it is fulfilling its plight
To bring joy and color to man
And be a part of God's sweet plan.

I Love That You Love Me

My son and I always express our love
In a cute and whimsical way
It's usually with "a bushel and a peck"
And "hugs and kisses around the neck"
And that really starts our day.

Well this morning I caught him off guard
As I told him "I love that you love me"
I think it sent him for a little twirl
Or rocked his mighty world
But a twinkle in his eyes I did see.

It's not belittling to show your love
Or even give a hug or two
Even Christ showed us while on the cross
With arms stretched out He reached across
To say, "This much I love you."

For God so loved the world that He gave His only begotten Son...
John 3:16

God Is So Good

God is an awesome God
He's so good to me
He knows my needs and wants
And where I need to be.

Turmoils and trials come my way
But He is always by my side
He has never given up on me
Within my heart he abides.

He has led me through green pastures
And down dark and lonely roads
He's been there through rough storms
And lifted many heavy loads.

He's with me in the morning
He's with me at noon day
And even in the evenings
He will never go away.

School Daze

School days, school daze
Well, the time is almost here
Getting touch with old friends
Facing anticipation and a little fear.

Walked into my 5th grade classroom
Sat at my desk - row 4 seat 5
Kept looking at the cutest boy
Then suddenly I caught his eye!

Greeted him with a little wave
And a bashful, uncommon smile
As time passed we began to talk
Then friendship grew stronger for quite a while

As time went on, we knew each other well
Began to whisper out loud, got a little careless
Teacher caught us "jabber jawing"
Had to write on chalkboard, I Will Not Talk In Class.

Well this was just a beginning I thought
Of a friendship that would last forever
When at our high school graduation
He wrote in my yearbook something clever.

Continued next page

He had asked me a question to my surprise
"Remember first grade...I do?"
Nothing came to mind so I asked him "what?"
He shyly replied, "That's when I liked you!"

Twelve long years we had grown up together
Laughing and skating, just getting along
Then each one went their separate ways
Not forgetting a childhood memory so strong!

Well, where ever you are dear friend of mine
Just let the truth be known to you
If I could go back and write in your yearbook that day
I simply would have said, "I liked you too."

Twelve long years we had grown up together
Laughing and skating, just getting along
Then each one went their separate ways
Not forgetting a childhood memory so strong!

<u>Dancing Horses</u>

Dancing horses prancing round and round
Moving graciously as they jump up and down,
Music is playing to calm these gentle beast
They are well behaved to say the least!

A pretty platform decked with many shades
And mirrors to enhance the escapades
With strings of beautiful colored lights
Makes for the riders an exciting sight.

"Carousel Waltz" the tune doth play
To add a touch of magic to the day
Making everything seem so real
Oh the wonder of the "Carousel."

Been a while since the music has played
Guess it's being reserved for a special day
Once it was given from a special friend
Maybe one day it will play again.

Trust

When at my very lowest
Trust was what I needed
Couldn't find it in my heart
Not a suggestion was heeded.

Then one day it came to me
As I traveled toward my home
God was sending messages
"My child, you're not alone."

"Trust in the Lord with all thine heart"
Were the messages that were seen
From a little tag with PROV 3:56
To two church display screens.

So I started listening to the Lord
As doubt and fear gave in
Knew I had found my answer...
Knew I had found my friend.

Today trust is a constant companion
And God a trusted friend
I know that He'll be with me
Until my very end.

Trust in the Lord with all thine heart and lean not on your own understanding. In all thy ways acknowledge Him and He will direct thy path. Prov 3:5,6

© 08/13/2019, Alinda C Daniels

<u>Any Day Now</u>

My Lord could come any day now
I believe this with all my heart
He's gone to make a place for us
So we could never from him depart.

In the Bible, true word of God
He tells me of a land so fair
Where we'll never grow old
And we'll join our loved ones there.

But until that wonderful day
When we are gathered home
Just look toward the east
That's where He'll come from.

His arrival will be exciting
Unbeknownst to anyone
And when He leaves with all his children
His victory has been won!

So stand alert for that special day
For it will come without any mention
Be ready for your glorious day
Of a grand heavenly ascension.

Christ could come at any moment. I believe that with all my heart—not because of what I read in the newspapers, but because of what I read in Scripture.
John F. MacArthur

© 08/08/2019, Alinda C Daniels

Peace Not War

Woodstock was at different time and place
A time of peace...not a war to face.
There was singing and dancing among a field
And draft dodgers not wanting to kill.

Living through this time in '69
Some were dreading to face the line
Woodstock was so free and alive
But soldiers in Vietnam were trying to survive.

Woodstock was a time of laughter and cheer
In my world it was a time of tears
Woodstock meant meeting new friends often
In mine, seeing friends come home in coffins.

It's true I was angry that they were free
And just singing "Let It Be, Let It Be"
Cause we were busy fighting a war
And begging for it to be o'er.

To bring Woodstock back would be a mistake
It's over and done, no need to debate
Let's get along with the time we are in
And everyone, everywhere just be friends.

<u>Issaqueena Falls</u>

The Legend of Issaqueena Falls:

The Cherokee were ready to attack the settlements on the upper South Carolina frontier. Issaqueena, a young Cherokee maiden, leaped upon her fastest pony to warn them of their fear of coming attacks. She travelled for 96 miles around the area and made many points of contact for which small towns of South Carolina were named. Fearing retribution from the Cherokees, Issaqueena stayed with Allan Francis, a trader at one of the settlements

The Cherokee Chief, angry with the white settlers, decided to send his warriors after her. Issaqueena saw them coming and ran towards the falls. Knowing that the Cherokee believed that evil spirits were living in the waterfalls, she pretended to leap to her death. It is said that she hid on the ledge below the top of the waterfall where she remained until it was safe to rejoin her family eventually marrying Allan Francis.

In time, she, Allan, and their newborn baby moved back to Stumphouse Mountain where they built their home.

Issaqueena Falls, near Walhalla, South Carolina, is a 200 ft high cascade waterfall in the Oconee District of the Sumter National Forest. Stumphouse Mountain tunnel is the remains of an 1850s attempt to link the port of Charleston to the cities of the Midwest by rail. The Civil War brought the construction to an end.

Fear The Feelings

Fear...a compelling little word
It can appear in times of trouble
Maybe even while we sleep
Or it could never, at all, be heard
And never give a peep.

It's there in a voice when two collide
Or when faced with a dangerous situation
Even in a bad dream at night
It's just a feeling deep inside
That you can't possibly keep quiet.

Sometimes it appears in a split second
And expressed in a minute or two
Or sometimes it's around several days
While within the heart it beckons
Please, please goes away.

It can be in the form of rejection
And the fear of just saying "No"
Or in the thrill of your heart at play
Just face your fears with anticipation
And live to fear another day.

Goodnight Baby Girl

August 16, 2006 - a day to remember
Much unlike that 3rd day in December
When you were born and the angels sang
Only time can heal this lonely pain

You see God decided you'd be leaving
But no more time left for grieving.
It's been fifteen years since you've been gone
And it's really good to know you're home.

You see, Baby Girl, I had you for a while
I was blessed with your beautiful smile
Now God is reaping all His rewards
And you've received your heavenly awards.

It's never good to say goodbye
But no more sorrow, I'll try not to cry
I'll hold you in my heart for keeps
Just knowing you're having a blissful sleep.

Goodnight, sweet dreams m Baby Girl
Yea the one with the soft, golden curls
'Tis time to lay you down to sleep
And forever your memories I will reap.

<u>Yesterdays Remembered</u>

Memories seem to fervently rush in
Of you my lover and my friend
It's been a bright and sunny day
But storms seemed to come my way.

It started out to be so swell
But tears in my eyes begin to swell
Thoughts rush in, feeling the loneliness
While listening to our favorite songs I guess.

It's been a while since you've been gone
I've had this yearning for so long
And, oh, how I miss you loving arms
That kept me from any pain or harm.

I miss our dance across the floor
And the way you walked through the door
I loved the way you said, "Hello"
And how mischievously your smile did show.

I miss the "dates" we use to go on
And the gentleman way you had shown
You were so shy I finally realized
Which was to me a great surprise.

Your soothing voice, your kiss so dear
Let me know I'm glad you were here
But now my love you have gone
And I am feeling so alone.

The Wedding

It was a beautiful Saturday night
In a quaint country church filled with light
When two people were to become as one
Yes the wedding ceremony had just begun.

The couple were up front with Pastor O'Lear
Yes he had lots for them to hear
"Do you take this person" he said
They both said "Yes" and nodded their head

Next the exchanging of the rings
Both beautiful and meaningful things
No beginning or end signifies life
Of the marriage between a husband and wife.

And now the announcement heeded for life
"I now pronounce you Man and Wife!"
Finally the climax no one would miss
When the Pastor said you two can kiss!

Moonlight On The Lake

Busy day at the lake with fishing
And a picnic around the banks
Sitting here hoping and wishing
Giving the good Lord all our thanks.

It's been a fun-filled day of joy
With sharing all our love
Topped off with perfect weather
Sent to us from up above.

But now the day is winding down
And the day's events must close
I'll never forget this one remarkable day
And this special place we chose.

Now as I sit and reminisce
About a day being so great
I'm in awe of God's great wonders
As I view the moonlight on the lake.

<u>Inside Out</u>

Have you ever been in a hole
That you just can't seem to get out
Or does it seem you just sit
And stir and fume and pout?

It's a lonely place to be in
No one to understand
Where and when did it all begin
I'd like to take a stand.

The walls seem to close in on me
In silence I'm getting deaf
I feel the coldness when you talk
I see it on your breath.

It's not that I want to be this way
A stranger I've become
Not wanting to get out and associate
I'm "happy" in my home.

Just put me on a shelf somewhere
Forget that I'm around
Don't bother trying to turn a smile
From an upside frown.

Being A Mom

Being a mom is really tough
When going through hardships
And the going gets rough.
It isn't easy to just say no
When faced with obstacles
And giants that suddenly show.

It's tough being an auto tech
When your car you're driving
Seems to have a wreck.
It's tough being counselor and friend
And a mom at the same time
And try to find the beginning or end.

It's never easy being on call
24/7
But I will be there through it all.
You see, being a mom is truly a blessing
No doubt about it
You're worth it all without any guessing.

<u>Momma's Hands</u>

Momma's hands were gentle and strong
In times they let me know when I did wrong
But they were always there to teach me things
And help me by any means.

They worked with pride on a job well done
And always tried to be number one
They taught me the essentials of life
They worked long hours and with great strife.

Momma's hands were there when I'd fall
To lift me up from a crawl
To give me hope to go on
To know I would never be alone.

Her hands always seem so giant to me
Guess it took me a while to see
That they were covering me with grace
And no one could ever take her place.

Make It All Go Away

Make it all go away
There's too much to bare
Too much to think about or say
Too much to even care.

Words passed without a thought in mind
To be remembered no more
But the ways of this are so unkind
And left an open sore.

The load is weighted down too much
Seems more than I can handle
Time to lift the load as such
Going to bind them in a bundle.

Gonna lift the heavy boulders
With all my strength and faith
And throw them from my shoulders
And be satisfied with God's grace!

God's Caring Angels

God bless those loving angels
Who care and heal the sick and needy
They are the health care workers
And of their time, they're not greedy.

Their work cannot go unnoticed
As they work long hours into the night
We compliment them for their knowledge
To determine between wrong or right.

Yes, they're there anytime we need them
And we thank them for their time
God grant them good health in return
And give them peace of mind.

The Palmetto State

Welcome to South Carolina
A place you'll want to vacation
From the beautiful Blue Ridge Mountains
To the coast with the mighty Atlantic Ocean.

There's Charleston waiting just for you
So full of interesting themes
Like Rainbow Row, The USS Yorktown...
And beauty and history beyond your dreams.

A lot of adventure for everyone to do
Like take a carriage ride or go on a ghost hunt
Or visit some of the historical churches
And learn how we survived the soldier's blunts.

Yes, there was Blackbeard and England
Wanting to capture the region
But eventually came the Civil War
At which Charleston surrendered her legion.

Continued next page

She has survived wars and hurricanes
And earthquakes as such
But she held on to her dignity
And shows it in her gracious touch.

Rainbow Row is a famous attraction
With thirteen multi-colored Georgian houses
Merchants' businesses in the lower part
And the upper part was enjoyed by spouses.

The "slave market" is an open market
Where one can buy souvenirs
And pubs and restaurants of many kinds
Are waiting for the patrons here.

South Carolina has fought her battles
Now raises her flag with pride
She's one of thirteen colonies
And yes, she survived!

The Song

Have you ever started out feeling fine
Having a great day, maybe having some wine
Then a song comes on the radio
And your body trembles and you let go
Of feelings of love you once shared
With someone, your soul you bared?

The song was special as we danced that night
Everything was so special and right.
A song of yesterday - an oldie you might say
But a special one I'm glad they played.
It brought back memories of my past
Memories that I wished had last.

But never will it just be a song
It's a song in my heart where you belong.
It's a mark in my mind, a cherished thought
Of emotions that can never be bought.
It's brings a warm and loving smile
As I hear "Rest Your Love On Me A While."

Dancing Feet

Gonna put on my dancing feet
Gonna dance across the floor
Gonna throw myself a party
Gonna remember you no more.

Come and join the celebration
And dance the night away
Get in touch with the music
As you swing and sway.

Try a Texas two-step
Or do a little shuffle
Just do it as you feel
Without the frills and ruffles.

Move your feet, feel the thrills
As the music stirs your soul
Join in the dance party
All you young and old.

Listen to the music
Pick up on the beat
Get yourself a swinging
And move those dancing feet.

Days The Music Died

From JFK in '63 which was beyond belief
There's been too many tears and a lot of grief
So much has happened and too often it seems
And many years of broken dreams.

Time of disasters one cannot fix
Like the Challenger in '86
When lives of seven innocent ones were lost
And everyone felt the pain it cost.

With the loss of Diana in '97
To the loss of The Towers on 9/11
I've had several "Days the Music Died"
Cannot count the tears I've cried.

But life goes on as it did before
With tragedies happening galore
I'm not keen to today's situation
Too much to expect with any anticipation.

All days mentioned were "worst" days at the time, but my heart really went out for the members of the Space Shuttle Challenger and the country. This, probably, was the worst "DAY The Music Died" for me.

<u>My Tractor</u>

Gonna ride my tractor
All over the place
Not gonna be in a hurry
And not gonna be in a race.

Got me a new John Deere
A truly great machine
Has many neat compartments
Makes me feel like I am king.

Can rustle up all the animals
And lead them to the barn
Will ride to the garden
Or plow up all the farm.

Yep, gonna ride my John Deere
And put it to the test
To see if it will beat all others
And be the very best!

Dad and I are now alike
We both have our favorite toys
To keep us quite busy
And make us happy boys.

No Matter How Old

I guess it's a natural instinct
To worry about one's own
When times are so unpredictable
And life is so unknown.

I sit and wait so patiently
But the time still goes on
My heart is anxiously waiting
For a child of mine to come home.

The darkness has crept in like a thief
And more thoughts of fear fill my mind
Don't want to think the worst of things
Trying to put them all behind.

Start my usual prayer session
To calm this troubled one
God is really there to listen
He'll help the wandering son.

Hold My Hand

Hold my hand, oh Lord I pray
Help me through another day
Help me face what lies ahead
Take away this fear and dread.

Stand beside me, make me strong
Protect me when things go wrong.
Reassure me that you are here
All your love to me endear.

Give me strength to carry the load
Walk with me down this bumpy road
Pick me up when I slip and fall
Remind me Lord, you can handle all.

Thank you for your loving arms
That protects me from all harm
Your tender touch I am aware
That you have me in your care.

For I the LORD thy God will hold thy right hand, saying unto thee, Fear not; I will help thee. Isaiah 41:13 KJV

Sunday Delight

Sunday midday in the park
Picnic on a grassy knoll
Bottle of white wine to touch
My heart and my inner soul.

Such a beautiful place to pick
No better place than this
We shared each other's moments
And sealed them with a kiss.

We reminisced of many good times
Spoke very little of the bad
Remembered old friends from the past
And the loss of some made us sad.

But here we are in the present time
You and me alone together
Enjoying each other's company
Not worrying about the weather.

Suddenly, out of the crystal blue
Comes a classic springtime rain
Drenched us both through and through
Back to the present we seem to regain.

Just another precious memory
To add to our book of treasures
Of the picnic, the romance and the RAIN
And laughter beyond measure!

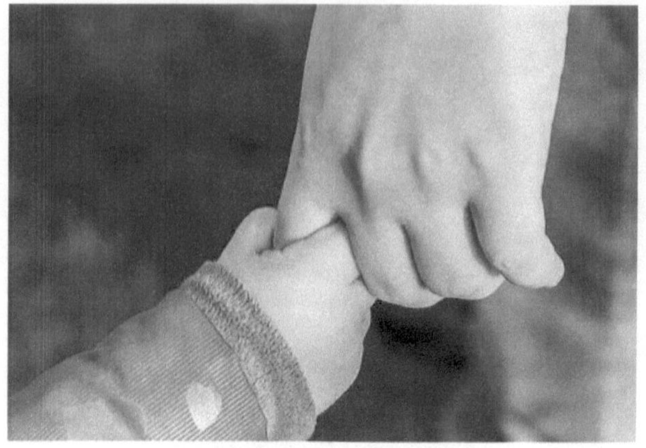

Don't Let Go

When I stumble or if I fall
Protect me from the blow
Gently hold me in your arms
------ And Don't Let Go.

When I am down to a crawl
The going seems so slow
Help me take those perfect steps
------ And Don't Let Go.

When times get rough
And I'm at my low
Please don't give up on me
------ And Don't Let Go.

Be there in triumphant times
Set my heart aglow
Take me by your gentle hands
------ And Don't Let Go.

The Tough Go Shopping

Have you ever heard the saying...
"When the going gets tough, the tough go shopping!"
Well, that's the perfect remedy
So off to town I'm hopping.

Guess I'll hit my favorite Wal-Mart
To see what I can find
Gonna go from back to front
And wait in long, long lines.

Next to Michael's - a neat variety store
Where I can get some crafts and things
My spare time to fill up
And see what Christmas brings.

Now to my favorite "Mickey D's"
To grab a happy meal
Something simple yet so good
And quite a reasonable deal.

Guess it's time to head back home
To do what mom's do best
Take control of all the chores
And guard off all unwanted guests.

You see, there always another day
When the going gets tough...

The Phone Call

Got a phone call today
From someone special to me
Wanted me to give them room
And let them be who they want to be

So here's to your wishes
I grant them all to you
May you be what you want
And do what you must do.

Don't want to rustle up your hair
Don't want cause no grief
Just let me know that you're still here
And stay strong to your belief.

Gonna let you go your separate way
Won't hinder you a bit
But rest for sure if you're hurt
I'll truly pitch a fit!

Just call me if you need me
I'll always return your call
I'll be there in a minute
Goodbye my dear, that's all.

<u>Old Glory</u>

I remember the good old school days
When we saluted the American flag
No one thought it was unconstitutional
No one thought it was a drag.

We placed our hands across our chest
We raised our heads with pride
We felt a love for our country
And peace deep inside.

But times have changed in our country
And the flag is under constant fire
A lot of folks can't or won't spread
This need for American desire.

They'd rather rip and tear the flag
Or burn it from a stake
The flag was once called "Old Glory"
But now it's taken as a mistake.

No one seems to honor her colors
Over the battle grounds she hovered
No one gets this final respect
Except when laid to rest well covered.

Don't trample on this symbol of strength
Raise your heads and hands
Just remember this symbol of freedom
And let her fly across the land.

<u>Angel Wings</u>

I will lift you up on angel wings
Carry you across the sky
Take you to the Father's breast
Where you no longer will die.

To a place where joys never end
And tears are never known
Where peace is everlasting
A place you will call home.

You'll have so much love to share
And a crown upon your head
And riches beyond belief
In God's word it is read.

The Master stands there waiting
With loving arms opened wide
Just waiting for you His child
To welcome you inside.

He'll lift you up on angel's wings
To take you directly to His home
Where you shall evermore be there
And nevermore to roam.

The Store Window Lady

While walking through the city
I noticed several shops
With store front windows
And most amazing props

But only one caught my eye
The one beside the tall, dark stranger
She looked so elegant and meek
As if no one could rearrange her

Her hair was harvest brown
Not one hair out of place
And her lips were deepest pink
That spread joy all over her face.

Her dress was a white chiffon
That flowed so elegantly
With tiny rosettes on the bodice
That matched her to a tee.

Her shoes were satin white
And they fit her just fine
Her tiny foot stood on the floor
They were a size divine.

In her hand a bouquet of roses
That she carried with pride
Her joys for this day
She definitely could not hide.

Then I watched as someone took her
Out of the window front that day
The store window lady had gone
And took my dreams away.

<u>Strike Up The Band</u>

It's Friday night football time
And the hometown team is here
Along with a crowd of folks
To greet them with a cheer.

Among the crowd of folks
Is the favored high school band
That is essential to the team
To show them they are grand.

The team is moving toward the goal
And the band is playing "The Horse"
The excitement seems to elevate
And they score again, of course.

Now it's halftime and it's time
To strike up the band and perform
So they march with heads held high
Across the field in perfect form.

Throughout the game they've played
Their songs of cheer and praise
To support their team and home
Throughout the coming days.

They're done for the night's event
And done their task quite well
Now it's time for them to exit the field
And go to where they dwell.

Can You Hear?

Can you hear the rustle of angel wings
Or feel their brush across your face?
Do you ever wonder how they show up
In the most needed place?

They're there in times of danger
And they guide us from above
They're God's most treasured messengers
Sent from Him with all His love.

Can you hear the small voice calling
Within your inner heart?
Do you listen to the message
Or do you from it depart?

It's the tender voice from The Father
Speaking to you alone
Seeking your heart and soul
Helping you become strong.

Take time to listen for the rustle
And hear that sweet, sweet voice
It's never too late for you
To make that final choice.

God is in His kingdom
And He's waiting for your call
Just open up your heart
And give unto Him your all.

<u>God's Speed</u>

God's speed in everything you say
And in all you choose to do
Truly know that He is always
Watching over you.

He's with you in the morning
And even at noon's light
He's with you in the evening
And all during the night.

Rest assure you aren't alone
In this world of sin
Make sure you have the promise
And Christ you have let in.

Stay strong in what you believe
The battle sometimes gets rough
But God is always in the midst
And you just have to stand tough.

God's speed when you are weary
And you need a place to rest
You'll have a place to go to
It's in the Father's breast.

Olden Times

As I sit here in the quiet room
I watch him play a video racing game
And I think back to my childhood
Where nothing was the same.

We use to play outdoors a lot
No electronic games we had
We'd play chase or hide 'n seek
And if we got caught, it was too bad.

We'd play around the big oak tree
Cowboys and Indians was the test
We'd laugh and holler oh so loud
And try to see who was the best.

Then we'd hear the ice cream truck
Coming down the street
And we'd run and get our quarter
And off to it we'd greet.

Yes these were much simpler days
When everything was great
And all the children could play
Without facing a possible fate.

Sometimes I wish for olden times
But know that it can't be
So I sit here watching him
Beat the car in front of me.

<u>Stairway To Heaven</u>

I wish there was a stairway
That I could actually climb
I'd gladly take the journey
To go to a place so divine.

It might take me a while to get there
But I feel it's not too far
Can't get there by walking
Or even in a car.

But I know that it does exist
'Cause the Bible tells me so
It speaks of pearly gates
And streets of purest gold.

This place called Heaven
Is but a breath away
But only can you get there
When you've seen you final day.

No ladder can I climb
To get me to this place
It's awfully hard to wait
To meet God face to face.

But I know that I'll take the trip
I've waited here patiently to go
I know I am going there
My God has told me so.

God Is Everywhere

God Is Everywhere,
Just look around and see
He's in the sunshine and the rain
And all things wild and free.

He's in the air we breathe
And in the things we touch
He's is in the skies and the earth
And the things we care for so much.

He's next to you when you're sleeping
Or riding down the road
Or when you are troubled
And have a heavy load.

He's with you when you're joyful
Or overwhelmed with tears
He's there through your burdens
Or facing unknown fears.

He's waiting to hear you say
You're sorry for the wrong you've done
Accept His love and forgiveness
And accept Jesus as the only Son.

<u>Sunday Dinner</u>

On Sundays everyone would gather
At momma and daddy's house to eat
We'd have quite an enormous feast
Followed with a sweet treat.

Momma usually had fried chicken,
Mashed potatoes and green beans
Along with other fixins
Brought by other means.

Then someone would take a notion
To make a churn of cream
That's what we all decided
That was the children's dream.

So when the cream was frozen
Daddy tool the dasher out
Then everyone had their share of cream
Taking turns about.

Now everyone had their fill
Of dinner and a treat
Next to the front porch we did go
To have a relaxing and needed retreat.

A Day To Remember

On September 11, 2001, I was sitting at work
Doing my job until I heard some terrible news
Heard a news flash on my radio
Planes had flown into the towers in New York
And next to the pentagon they did go.

Seem like all the workers were shocked
No one seemingly interested in work
Wondering how this could possibly happen
Soon we knew our nation had been rocked
The spirit of America had been dampened.

Too many lives were lost that day
From those in the commercial aircraft
To the ones in the towers
To military troops fighting this cause far away
And first responders rescuing for hours.

Well, later that day when I finally got home
This tragedy was all over tv
So much heartaches, disasters and pain
People were scattered with no place to roam
And so many could never go home again.

September 11 will always be 9-1-1 to us all
A day of an ultimately, inconceivable tragedy
But it is a day remembered with grief
A day when America had an awakening call
But She will be a survivor, that is our belief.

<u>Tomorrow</u>

If only we could know
what tomorrow would bring
We'd do the things we put aside
And do our favorite things.

We'd take our time
Not rushing about
And smell the roses
Which we forgot, no doubt.

We'd listen to the music
And dance to the tune
Of joyful spring time
As a warm day in June.

We'd pay attention
To those we love
And seek the guidance
From God above.

We'd thank God
Who is so merciful
For tomorrow's day
We'd be so grateful.

Take tomorrow as a given
In everything you do
It is a blessing from above
Given directly to you.

<u>Angels</u>

Angels are among us
With every breath we take
In every waking moment
And every move we make.

They're with us in the morning
At noon time and at eve
In every season of the year
And with us when we grieve.

They're never so far away
That they cannot answer a call
When times are troubling
They there amongst us all.

They're in the clouds
Awaiting so very patiently
They're always there
They will always be.

Angels are among us
Don't you ever forget
Might be a day you'll need them
Don't make it a regret.

Time

Time is of the essence
Time never stands still
It doesn't wait for no man
It isn't in a will.

Time is of the future
And never is reversed
It's there for you to take
And never to be cursed.

Make the most of time you have
Enjoy each second given to you
Know not when you breathe your last
Or when your account is due.

You only have one life to live
So make the most of it
Don't let it slip away from you
While you just give up and sit.

Remember time is of the essence
Don't run and try to hide
It's part of your make up
Which affects you deep inside.

To Those That Fell

They were in their prime
When God called them home
They had given up their time
To go to a foreign place all alone.

They answered the call so bravely
From their favorite nesting place
They joined hundreds so gravely
Facing the enemy face to face.

With hearts pounding within their chest
They faced the murky mire
And one would kneel to the test
When hit with enemy fire.

The loss of those so young in years
In a land so strange and far away
Have brought home a million tears
And still do to this very day.

To those who served at his due
And gave their very best
Much appreciation goes out to you
You've passed the ultimate test.

Greater love hath no man than this, that a man lay down his life for his friends. John 15:13

© 09/16/2019, Alinda C Daniels

Knocking On Heaven's Door

It seems like my favorite bush
That blooms this time of year
Is the beautiful blue hydrangea
The blossoms bring to me a tear.

I remember my mama's loving touch
As she nursed each delicate part
Sometimes she gave a little nudge
She always worked with all her heart.

She gave me a cutting from the bush
As I nursed it with great strife
It's a remembrance of a special time
That she shared with me in life.

Today I can picture her beside the bush
As those days are all forgone
Knowing that when season ends
The blossoms would soon be gone.

Still as the plants go dormant
And the blossoms cease no more
These beauties will be revived again
Knocking on heaven's door.

Saved By Grace

I've traveled along on a wrong turn
Been so alone my insides churn
But God had things under control
And by grace I was made whole.

It was by faith His works were seen
And by His grace I was made clean
The Father had His hand on me
Now I'm living proof, I'm free.

You see, my failures that I have done
Have been erased, thank God I've won
He guards me like a child at play
Covers me both night and day.

Salvation is God's gift to us all
We must answer when He calls
Ready to spread His wonderful love
That is freely received from above.

Just remember our faith is the key
Of being saved, of being set free
God's grace will always see you through
You'll feel refreshed as the morning dew.

Never forget: We are saved by grace through faith, not by works. Our salvation, and our ministry, is the gift of God (Ephesians 2:8-10).

Remember that failure is an event, not a person….Zig Ziglar

<u>St. Matthew's Evangelical Church</u>

Made a trip to Charleston, SC
To trace my family tree
Visited St. Matthew's Church
Was so beautiful to me.

Gave me cold chills
As I silently stepped inside
Made me so proud
So full of peace and pride.

The alter was a solemn place
Within an arched dome
A large stained glass of Christ
Highlighted this sacred home.

A home where my ancestors
Once worshipped and sang His praise
And now I felt the feelings
Of their yesterdays.

The Oconee Bell

The Oconee Bell is a tiny wildflower
Growing along the Jocassee streams
Poised in pure and elegant array
Awakening as if from a night's dream.

Once named "Acony" by the Cherokee
Later the name was changed
When an explorer discovered it in 1787
And the name "Oconee" was obtained.

It grows in the wild desolate places
Along mountain streams and banks
It isn't a collectible or a souvenir
It's of the endangered rank.

It's flower is made of petals of five
Ranging from white to rose purple
And the center ovary is a yellow hue
Colors that are quiet subtle.

A bell-shaped flower flaring
As the sepals add to the flower's view
The blossom usually nods notably
At the point where the petals fuse.

The Weather

Rain today without a doubt
Tomorrow much the same
For the weekend we'll have some sun
That's what the weatherman proclaims.

The weekend is beautiful outside
No rainfall is in sight
Temperature is rising too hot
Even in the middle of the night.

Next day the clouds are heavy
As the raindrops began to fall again
Looks like the rain will linger a while
According to the weatherman's plan.

The weather is forever changing
But it changes per God's request
No need for fuss or complaining
The weather's already been set.

Maybe during all these changes
Something magnificent will show
Maybe a symbol that all is ok
When God sends us a rainbow!

The Pain I Bare

I need not hide the pain I bare
Nor put it on a shelf
But somehow, some way
I keep it to myself.

I fear that someday I will fail
To keep the feelings in
And burst out with all the pain
To know not when to end.

The pressures of this life I have
Is like a cooker about to blow
It's not a feeling of relief
But one of a great plateau.

But on to another day I'll go
With hopes of great anticipation
Who knows not what tomorrow may bring
When facing a different situation.

<u>A Magic Lamp</u>

I wish I had a magic lamp
To make your wish come true
I'd wipe away your tears of despair
And grant this peace for you.

I'd rub it so heartedly until
It would grant a wish for thee
And make your every dream come true
But I know that just can't be.

It's just a ordinary lamp
Of copper, brass or silver
It doesn't even take requests
Nor does it ever quiver.

The only thing this lamp can do
Is dress a coffee table
I rub it when I'm polishing it
But no magic becomes enabled.

<u>Sidewalk Watching</u>

I sat outside in my car today
While my grandson had an meeting
'Twas really an interesting adventure
As I watched people leaving.

One man had left the office building
And sat on the outside bench
He evidently was talking to himself
His facial expressions he would wrench.

Just then a group of four met outside
On this cool September day
All of them patiently listened
As each girl had her say.

It seemed a meeting of great concern
While everyone frowned or nodded
But eventually they must have agreed
And to each one's car they trotted.

Could have been important
Or simply what's for lunch
In any case, the decision
Was needed made by this bunch.

Next a robust, purple haired young woman
Come busting out the door
Seems like she was so happy
To have completed this appointed chore.

It's really quite amazing
At all the different personalities
You can see them all the time
If you just stop, wait and see.

<u>God's Messengers</u>

Tiny Lil Angel sent with blessings from above,
To bring someone joy and fill their heart with love.
Bringing peace and tranquility to a troubled one,
Knowing not your mission until the job is done.

Tiny Lil Angel, you've come a long way
To help the weary through another long day.
You lift someone from a heavy load
You bring joy to someone sad it is told.

Tiny Lil Angel, you're such a pleasant sight to see
Your entertaining, joyful smile brings contentment to me.
I'm so glad you were sent to cheer me on
Otherwise, my days would be awfully long.

Tiny Lil Angel, you work with all your strife
You've brought a fulfillment to my life.
Thanks for the visit you made to me
I'll guard you gently, as gently as I can be.

The Quilt

There lays a covering on my grandma's bed
With a history behind it... it is said.
The young ladies use to gather and sew
And learn the gossip they didn't know.

Yes, it's true they'd have a quilting party
And their efforts were always quite hearty.
The patchwork squares were sewn that day
With cotton thread that would not fray.

A time of laughter to cry and to sing
Around the table, the quilt would bring.
A joyful peace for all who would gather
To remain as friends for ever and ever.

It seems the quilt was finished on time
To be a gift for someone so fine.
Tradition has it – a quilting party is said
To make a covering for a new bride's bed.

originally written 04/26/2019

<u>Listen To My Heart . . .</u>

Listen to my heart oh Mighty One
Hear my cries of despair
Touch me with your tender hand
Let me know you're really there.

Listen to the tears I cry
Wipe each drop from my cheek
Lift me up when I am down
Give me strength when I am weak.

Listen to my doubts and fears
That seems so out of control
Caress me with your gentle love
Keep me safe within your fold

Listen as I cast my problems
That shroud my days with pain
Lift my eyes toward the stars
Renew my faith again.

When the world looks down on me
Give me strength to go on
Place me where I need to be.
And lead me gently home.

originally written 4/8/2005

<u>Poetry - My Time</u>

You can read me like a book
And all you've got to do is take a good look
I'll express my feelings in the poetry I write
Sometimes into the late of night.

Poetry is my time to escape the hassle
To fly away to my enchanted castle
To face a moment of doubt and gloom
To go to my paper and not my room.

I write to express a moment of gladness
Or tell about some extreme sadness
Like losing a daughter and the horrible pain
And how the tears came down like rain.

Sometimes an old picture or report on tv
Will strike the thoughts within me
Such as the child who waved a sign in the air
Inspiring me to write, "Father, Are You There?"

It doesn't take much to jiggle my thinking cap
Sometimes I'll choose poetry over a nap
Just give me some paper and a pen
And watch out, I'm writing again!

<u>Childhood Games</u>

It's not unusual to see today's child at play
Sitting in front of a video game all day.
They know not the thrills of Hide 'N Seek
And closing your eyes, don't you dare peek.

Or playing cowboys and Indians around the big tree
Where you were the cowboy and the Indian was me.
Me with my arrows and you with your guns
We would try to catch each other but, oh, how we run.

With a broom stick for our horse
We'd gallop with all our force.
After chasing each other for what seemed like a mile
We would claim a truce and just rest a while.

Then on to bigger and better things
Like an old tire made into a swing.
Or hop scotch with nine squares to jump
Or, maybe a tea party given at lunch.

Yes, it's true the times have changed
No one plays my childhood games.

originally written 04/26/2019

My Day

I wake up in the morning light
After having a restful night
And much to my delight
I'm still here.

I wonder what the day will bring
On this sunny day in spring
Will I fret or will I sing
Oh I fear.

I cannot rule out a tear or two
When I'm feeling down or blue
It only happens in a few
Days of drear.

A day of laughter is a must
Today I promise not to fuss
Or even swear or cuss
Oh day of cheer.

Will do my best, I will not fear
My days to me, I hold so dear.

<u>With Outstretched Arms</u>

I'm in an awkward position
When faced with opposition
I know that I must love not hate
To enter that Heavenly gate.

To turn the other cheek is hard
And I must always be on guard
Of those who want to smear my name
Or say that I'm the one to blame.

But Christ says turn the other cheek
Be loving to those who are critique
Love your friends, your enemies too
Even those who turn on you.

A stranger, a sister, friend or a brother
There can never be no other
Greater than the one who first loved us
For our sins, His death was a must.

He turned the other cheek that day
And never ever walked away
Upon the cross with outstretched arms
He'll rescue you from any harm.

When God Whispers Your Name

When God Whispers Your Name from above.
I know I'm losing my only true love
My only reason for living
Always on the end of giving.

Once you held me in your arms so tight
Made me safe and warm at night.
Never boasting, such a humble man
Always seeking God's plan.

Now you're entertaining angels
And spreading your joys and jangles.
Just want the best for thee
Want you to be happy and free.

I love you more today than yesterday
Even though you're away.
I can feel your presence so very near
To reminisce brings a tear.

Miss our lazy afternoons
Just isn't fair you left so soon.
Now I know you're free from any pain
My loss is truly God's gain.

God's Gifts For A Little While

I wonder what you would look like
If I could see you today
Would I recognize you, my siblings
If you should come across my way.

Would you be tall like daddy
With hair as black as coal
Would you have a sweet disposition
And a lot of self-control?

Or would you be like momma
With hair the color of brown
And know when you've done wrong
By her distinguished frown?

Continued next page

And would you have their love
That you inherited at birth
Would you share it with someone
With whom you felt their worth?

Would you be contented
With the person you've become
Or would you lose your integrity
And forget where you come from?

Oh yes, you were a gift
From our Father up above
You were here only for a short time
And returned on wings of a dove.

Tribute to Michael Troy and Sheila Ann, my brother and sister who died shortly after birth. God has them in His care.

© 04/20/2021, Alinda C Daniels

Springtime Fun

Sitting on my front porch
And swinging in my favorite swing
Listening to the music
As a robin in an oak tree sings..

He's got a strong opponent
As a blue jay comes his way
Passing through a dogwood tree
Where our cat wants to play.

I notice the gold in the daffodils
As they are spreading everywhere
I cannot not forget the beauty of the amarillas
As they share their fragrance in the air.

Oh how sweet to see a hummingbird
Fleeting across a red rose bush
Can't let our game of croquet
Scare him off in a rush.

Time to greet some evening friends
To enjoy a steak and red potatoes dinner
And end it with a rhubarb pie
Gosh, I hope it's a winner.

To top this day off I think we'll play S
Some good old fashion horse shoes
And later we'll all sit by a nighttime fire
And listen to some Ray Charles blues

Life Of The Tin Man

Sometimes the tin man had it made
Because he had no heart
He couldn't feel the tunes that played
That tore my heart apart.

He couldn't hear the lovely sound
Of music to my ear
He couldn't hear the guitar's pound
That brought a million tears.

He could only see in front of him
What was really on display
He couldn't see the hurt of them
Who were having a terrible day.

He couldn't have his soul in touch
With matters from the heart
Because he couldn't care so much
For he was set apart.

'Twas a loss to the tin man
To go without these things
But, in a way, he's a lucky fan
To pass what pain they bring.

<u>The Stone Was Rolled Away</u>

Remember the stone was rolled away
And everyone had wondered how
It was put there to permanently stay
Removing it would not be allowed.

Christ was laid to rest in this tomb
No way for Him to get out
But on the third day He left this room
And arose beyond any doubt.

Mary Magdalene was first to see the stone
As she came to visit the site
She feared for something wrong
Had happened during the night.

"Where had they taken my Lord," she cried
To a stranger she did not recognize
She had witnessed that her Lord had died
But He was alive, much to her surprise.

To the others, the news had spread
Of the miracle happening on this day
The Lord had risen, He's not dead
And the stone was rolled away.

Patience

One day while working on matters from the heart
I got a call from someone who wanted to be a part.
We talked a long, long time; the offer sound so good
Took a blind leap of faith, didn't know where I stood.

Well, calls kept coming and conversations were long
The callers were persistent and the speeches were strong.
I kept on listening and saying, "I don't know
The cost is too steep for me to go."

The voices were so encouraging and truthful, you see
I'll help you, just trust me, so, let's let this be.
I finally said yes to the offer made
But now I'm feeling overwhelmed and afraid!

What if the items sell or maybe they won't
I'll be in a world of hurt and that I don't want.
Let's just take it slow with the process
Then let's see if the project is a success!

Then maybe on to bigger and better things
Maybe on to fulfilling my dream
Just give me some time, be patient with me
The future is out there, you will see!

originally written 5/2/2019

The Timepiece

A friend gave to me a ladies watch
To add to my collection
It's very old and I just wonder
Was it given to one in affection?

Wonder what that special one felt
As she received her precious gift
Was it given with much love
Did it set her heart adrift?

Perhaps it was for an anniversary
Or some other reminder of time,
Maybe a gift of goodbye
Of a love that was sublime.

Was it a hand-me-down
From a mother's jewelry chest
Or maybe left in a will
To which no one contest?

Oh the stories it could tell
If only a clue I could see
But maybe someday little hint
Will find it's way to me.

In Loving Memory

Your gentle face and patient smile
With sadness we recall.
You had a kindly word for each
And died beloved by all.

The voice is mute and stilled the heart
That loved us well and true.
Ah, bitter was the trial to part
From one so good as you.

You are not forgotten loved one
Nor will you ever be.
As long as life and memory last
We will remember thee.

We miss you now, our hearts are sore
As time goes by we miss you more.
Your loving smile and gentle face
No one can ever fill your vacant place.

originally written 7/23/1983

Glory On His Face

I can hear the Master calling
From a distant far away place
I can only imagine to my delight
The glory on His face.

I can almost see Him coming
To fill me with His wonderful love
To spread His glory and His grace
To prepare me for Heaven above.

I can almost feel His tender touch
As He approaches ever so near
I wait so impatiently, yet so calm
For the Master to appear.

I can finally see Him approaching
This journey is almost at an end
He looks at me so tenderly
And stretches out His nail scarred hands.

He talks with me so earnestly
About a journey we will take
When, at last, I shall see
That beautiful Heavenly Gate.

He speaks a goodnight prayer
And gently closes my eyes
He says when I wake up
I'll have a much awaited surprise.
Sweet dreams!

The Heart

The heart is not a plaything
The Heart is not a toy
But if you want it broken
Just lend it to a boy.

And after he has ended
With all his filth and shame;
He'll finish all he intended
And find a well-kept name.

(Original version written 06/23/1966)
Alinda Crenshaw

(Modified Version)

The heart is not a token
The Heart is not a toy
But if you want it broken
Just lend it to a girl or boy.

And after they have ended
With all their filth and shame;
They'll finish all that was intended
And you'll become the blame.

This world is very tricky you see
Filled with games of disbelief.
It's not a world where you can be free
So guard yourself from an anxious thief.

Just ask the Father up above
Who Listens to each prayer
To cover you with unending love
And make you most aware.

Home Sweet Home

I rode by my old homeplace
And memories started rushing in
The joys that I had shared with all
I wanted to go back and begin again.

To go back and play hide 'n' seek
Or catch lightening bugs at night
My sister, cousins, friends and I
Would play despite the absence of light.

This was a home for all my friends
From church and school alike
The doors were always open
No one did mom and dad dislike.

I can still see me in the swing
Negotiating with my dad
About cruising with my girlfriends
And his terms always made me glad.

Precious memories have I many
Of my home sweet home
And it remains a special place
No matter where I roam.

Temperature Rising

It was a nice Saturday morning
And we started our JUNGLE ADVENTURE
The RUGGED HIGHLANDS being covered with heavy UNDERGROWTH
Made me question my indenture.

As we journeyed through the TROPICS
We settled for ENCAMPMENT by a WATERFALL
It was SURROUNDED by SPRAWLING SNAKES
And all kinds of tiny creatures that crawled.

Upon waking up the next morning
LAWLESS CANNIBALS were all around
They took us into CAPTIVITY
And forced us to GODFORSAKEN grounds.

We thought we were doomed
To lose our heads to the chief PRIMATE
But suddenly there appeared a man
Known as TARZAN, the great.

He rode in on his ELEPHANT
And a COUGAR close behind
He and the chief GORILLAS
Seemed to agree and a treaty was signed.

We joyfully left the village
And headed for higher ground
We knew within our hearts and HEADS
That we were homeward bound!

Children Do Grow Up

A little baby is born today
Caressed with love and tears
So tender, young and innocent
Delivered with lots of cheers.

Soon he grows to be a toddler
A romping through the house
Jumping and kicking
And even tormenting the mouse!

Next comes those inquisitive years
When puzzles just won't do
Starts an experiment on his on
Just to scare the heck out of you.

Then there's puppy love
When Sally and Jane catch his eye
And it's heartbreak city
When they tell him goodbye.

Before you know it he's taken a wife
And starting a family of his own
Time to face the facts of life
And reap what he has sown.

A little baby is born today
Caressed with love and tears
So tender, young and innocent
Delivered with lots of cheers...

Stand Beside Me

Stand beside me when storms arise
Be there to dry my crying eyes
Put your arms around me tight
During a long and frightening night.

Stand beside me when there is pain
Help me, my faith regain
Encourage me more to trust in Him
Lighten my days when they are dim.

Stand beside me when times are fun
And show me that He's the only one
Guide me through a day of cheer
Let me know you'll always be here.

Stand beside me when my days are ore
Help me regain my strength once more
To bravely answer the Master's call
And give in to death when I befall.

Stand with me, Lord, don't make me wait
Hold my hand as I experience the date
Can hardly wait to see your smile
I've been waiting for quite a while.

The Purpose

Dear Lord, I know you have a purpose
But I don't know what it is
I can only know within my heart
But it seems to be a quiz.

I trust in all you say Dear Lord
And I'm trying to adhere
Just give me strength to see it through
And faith to keep you near.

I know that you are here Dear Lord
And will be here 'til the end
I know not what tomorrow will bring
But I know you'll be here until then.

So when this task is over Dear Lord
And I've done my very best
I pray that I have accomplished what you ask
And I know I've passed the test.

Proverbs 3:6 "Trust in the Lord with all your heart and lean not on your own understanding in all your ways submit to him, and he will make your paths straight."

<u>Sparky and Precious</u>

My two dachshunds are my pride and joy
Precious is a prissy girl - Sparky a husky boy
They both love to play with toys
And to watch them brings much joy!

They greet strangers as they enter the house
Their barks would even frighten the mouse
They're two of a pair, a female and a spouse
They wake me each morning with their rouse.

When it come meals, they too want to share
They wait very patiently to be seen there
But wait too long and they begin to glare
And give you that "poor puppy" stare.

They show their love as dogs sometimes do
Why, even Precious will howl, "I love you"
And Sparky can look so humble and blue
When he thinks his petting is overdue.

They're really two precious pets to me
Two best friends that will always be
When I'm down they set me free
Yes that's Sparky "Harley" and Precious "Abbey."

Raindrops

The angels cried that horrible day
When Jesus Christ had died
Their tears fell like raindrops
And God the Father hurt deep inside.

The angels cried tears of joy
When Christ arose anew
He entered into the kingdom
What a joyous and exciting debut.

Today I saw a single drop
Fall from a darkened sky
And I couldn't help but wonder
Why on the cross, He had to die?

But then I was reminded
Of that price He paid for me
So that I could be what He wanted
And the Father I could see.

So when I see the raindrops
Fall from a heavy cloud
I'm thankful for the angel's raindrops
And how richly I'm endowed.

Facing My Obstacles

When I am faced with obstacles
That are beneath my control
I give to God my worries
And with Him we both hold.

He helps me seek His trusting word
His word is encouraging and very kind
To get me through this worrisome time
And ease this troubled mind.

By trusting in God's Holy word
I have confidence within my heart
To make the right decisions
And throw worries apart.

Thank you God for showing me guidance
To look to you when worries come my way
You have such a peaceful understanding
And grace to allow me a blessed day.

<u>Me, Myself and My Computer</u>

I bought myself a computer
Thought I would join the evolution
Much to my surprise
It wasn't the solution.

I learned it had more sense than I did
Which burned me to a tee
Thought, oh girl, you'll learn this thing
Or fall down to your knees.

So much to learn, so much to do
Thinking it would never end
Finally got my letter typed
But now it says, "Hit send."

Finally found the send key
And got my letter sent
Only problem with this deed
Is I don't know where it went.

Think I master this the old way
And stick to pen and ink
Will accomplish this another day
When I can "computer" think.

The Day My Heart Went Silent

It was Aug 16, 2010, I was having a simple surgery. This day marked
the anniversary of my daughter's death so I had her on my mind. Family was
there for support. Surgery began and was going as planned when suddenly,
my heart went to sleep. I was experiencing Takosubu - The Broken Heart
Syndrome. I had died but during this time. I became aware of the surroundings...
I was lying under a bright light, a clean, white sheet in a sterile environment,
could hear doctors and nurses making remarks of death, I had shallow breathing,
low pulse, etc. Remember wanting to go on to Heaven to see everyone but
something was keeping me here. Next, I was sent to ICU until my vitals got better;
couldn't speak for a few days. Remember being emerged in a pool of water for several
days. Not sure what this was. I know God spoke to me that day in a most unusual way.

No More Tears

No more tears to wet the eye
God in Heaven....He will dry
He'll take away your fears and strife
Of what you've obtained during your life
And set you on a new path
And protect you with His wrath.

Just be faithful, strong and true
And God will always be there for you
Even in your weakest hour
You can feel God's mighty power.
Just listen for Him to softly speak
His promises He will truly keep.

Just lean on the Master to carry you a while
He'll pick you up with a warm, gentle smile
He'll lift you up in His strong, loving arms
Always ready to keep you from harm
Reach out to touch Him as close as midair
He's waiting for you to just meet Him there.

Though I walk in the midst of trouble, thou wilt revive me: thou shall
stretch forth thine hand against the wrath of mine enemies and thy
right hand shall save me.
The Lord will perfect that which concerneth me: thy mercy, O Lord,
endureth forever – forsake the works of thine own hands. Psalms
138: 7-8

A Happy Wanderer

When I grow up I think I'll be
A happy wanderer, wild and free
Traveling from place to place
Meeting everybody face to face.

Not a dull trip will I take
Going where I choose to make
Riding trains or hopping a bus
Won't be no problem, won't be no fuss.

Gonna travel to some brand new sites
Where the sky is filled with lights
Big brass bands that fill the streets
Happy people waiting to meet.

Maybe find a shop to ponder
To fill some time as I wander.
Will later settle down for a rest
Gonna keep going when I feel my best.

So many places and things to see
All of them waiting just for me.
After all is said and day is done
Think I'll close this chapter of fun.

Gonna start a brand new day
As I travel on my way
Another novel on my list to review
Today I travel to the zoo.

<u>Santa's On Vacation</u>

The toyshop is bustling
The elves are hustling
But Santa is nowhere around
The elves ask, "what's up?"
He's lost his getup
And decided to leave town.

"Oh dear," Mrs Clause exclaims
What could be the blame
Of this extraordinary exemption?
A much needed rest
To pass the test
Of holiday redemption.

He's still around
Not making a sound
He's checking the list twice
Gonna give out the toys
For all girls and boys
Even if naughty or nice.

Yes he's taking a break
Before that holiday date
When he travels all through the night
He's enjoying his time
In a place sublime
And soaking up the sunlight.

So, here's to your health
You jolly old elf
May your vacation be instilled
With a great life
Without any strife
And all your wishes be fulfilled.

Lost In Time

On August 16, 2006, my precious daughter died from kidney failure. Being a mother, made it extremely hard. My heart broke each time I visited her grave. But as time went on, I learned she had not only lived with her kidney failing but she was living in an abusive marriage. One day when I visited her, I grieved so hard that I felt my heart give way to the stress. Grief was taking it's toll. Little did I know that it would affect me later on. Well, on August 16, 2010, I had surgery. I knew what date it was so I had my daughter on my mind. While the doctors were operating, my heart just went to sleep. I had experienced Takotsubo, broken heart syndrome. I remember lying under a white sterile sheet with the brightest light shining on me. I could hear people talking about what would happen if my vitals did not improve. I remember longing for Heaven. I was transferred to the ICU, then to a private room where therapy began. Learn to do all the things I had learned from birth. Five months later, I left hospital...God just wasn't ready for me yet.

This was a very personal experience. Relive it in my mind constantly. Still asking why I survived??

Dreams

I had a dream the other night
So real it seem to be
Your face was in the spotlight
Looking straight at me.

You were sitting in your favorite seat
And I was nestled on your lap
You strum your fingers across my cheek
My heart you seemed to entrap.

We had our usual conversation
About how the day had went
We talked and talked for hours
The night was almost spent.

But suddenly you were gone away
But a rose was left behind
Oh why could you have not stayed
Just for a little more time.

I woke up in a bed of tears
Remembering all of our good times
Oh for a moment to share the years
When I was yours and you were mine.

But some sweet day we'll be as one
We'll be in a different scene
We'll hug and laugh and have some fun
Except it won't be in a dream.

Dreams seem so real. When you've lost someone, dreams are the closest things to reality - if only for a little while.

Midnight Moments

It seems to be a midnight moment
And my mind has gone to work
Instilling on this tablet
Some words or even some quirks.

The words come swiftly then disappear
Once here and then they are gone
Leaving behind some gentle thoughts
Of a love as solid as stone.

He came into my life one night
A prince was shown to me
I began to know him quite well
He was all he said he'd be.

A gentle man of average height
But taller than trees it seemed
Blue eyes and shady grey hair
He was all I ever dreamed.

He took my hand and said, "Let's dance"
So we strolled across the floor
"Just one more time," we said in chime
So we danced so slow once more.

The music stopped...the thoughts have ended
The midnight moment just didn't last
Perhaps another place and time
I can venture into the past.

© 11/06/2019, Alinda C Daniels

<u>God Sees All</u>

As a child, I was taught some important rules
Do unto others as you would have them do unto you
Don't even cheat or think about stealing
Just remember with whom you'll be dealing.

Mama always taught us God was watching
How we were acting and how we were talking
Don't tell a story and please don't lie
Be sure to always have an honest eye.

Remember to honor your dad and mom
Who holds you tenderly in their palm
Have no other God is the only path to go
Do not hurt anyone with a fatal blow.

Be good to others you meet along the way
If you can't say good, then there's nothing to say
Lend a helping hand to someone in need
Don't be greedy, do a good deed.

These are only a few of God's commands
For us to adhere to and understand
Be sure to show you love to others
God is watching you sisters and brothers.

The Lighthouse

As I look out at the lighthouse
I see a mighty stand
Directing, guiding, navigating
A ship about to land.

It warns of impending dangers
Like rugged coastal shores
It's red and white lights shine
Where one has gone before.

If it wasn't for the lighthouse
Where would the ships be?
They would be sailing lost and alone
In a perilous, dangerous sea.

The greatest lighthouse today
Is Jesus Christ The Lord
He guides and keeps us safe from harm
We cannot choose to ignore.

It's just the same with us today
We're like a ship at sea
We drift to and fro through life
With protection that we need.

But with Jesus as our Captain
We will not sail alone
He will guide us safely
As He leads us gently home.

I Am Never Alone

I am never alone
I have Jesus by my side
He's with me everywhere I go
He doesn't run and hide.

He's my companion when I'm down
Or feeling unworthy or unappealing
He'll cover me with His loving arms
And erase the pain I feeling.

He'll lift me up on eagle's wings
Set me high upon the mountain
Breathe into me the breath of life
Let me drink from nature's fountain.

You see, I am never alone
Jesus is with me every day
He's my constant companion
And He never goes away.

Me And Teddy

Just me and teddy
Lying in a field of dreams
Flowers growing everywhere
Endless so it seems.

Thought we'd take a little rest
And laugh and talk awhile
Think about the times we shared
And how he makes me smile.

He doesn't talk very much you see
But I can read his mind
He's really one of the bestest friends
A girl could ever find.

He's warm and cuddly, just a hug
Soft as cotton and very sweet
He always listens to my every word
He's never pretentious and always meek.

Yes, he's my teddy I must admit
Take him away And I'll have a fit!

And The Lord Cried

If only I could have dried His eyes
When He shed the tears that day
Upon that cruel rugged cross
Our Savior would surely lay.

He died for all who believes in Him
No doubter does He accept
He grieves for those who die without
Please let Him intercept.

It's the most important decision
You will ever make
Just remember Jesus loves
And Jesus does not forsake.

So take a look at yourself
To see just where you stand
Are you safe within the arms
And are you part of God's plan?

<u>And The Music Plays On</u>

I Listen to the whippoorwills
As they sing their lovely tune
Calling to their mate
In the month of June.

Just a touch of nature
On a sunny day
Chirping words unknown to me
In a delightful way.

His music has ceased for now
But nature still abounds
The chirping of a little squirrel
Has finally come around.

The rustling of the leaves
As he scampers for a nut
The nibbling away at his treat
But finally leaves in a quick strut.

And in the quietness, I begin to notice
The wind is whistling a happy tone
I sit and listen so patiently
As the music plays on and on.

© 11/09/2019, Alinda C Daniels

To Say Goodbye

I cannot find the words that fit
To say goodbye to you.
You've always been there for me
Now I don't know what to do.

You've been my Godsend and true friend
for many, many years
And now you're being taken away
And all I have are tears.

Please stay for just a little while
While I hold you to my breast
Give me one more chance
To put your memory at rest.

My life without you will be so null
My heart will break into a million pieces
I cannot say goodbye right now
Until this hurting ceases.

Perhaps we'll meet again some sweet day
Either here or on
Heaven's shore
Just remember my dear friend
I'll love you even more.

God's Speed!

Come Hither And See

Amazing things happen
When angels show up
As I can attest to a vision
As I saw her closeup.

She was standing in the doorway
As radiant as could be
When she spoke and said,
"Come hither and see."

She showed me a glimpse of Heaven
And said that's where you'll be
When you take flight
And it's your time to leave.

Well, her visit was short
But oh so reassuring
Makes life here
A little more enduring.

<u>Sisters</u>

Three sisters I have
Who are the best as can be
We laugh and cry together
And they let me be me.

We've had our up times
And had our down
But they are always there
When I need them around.

We each have our memories
Of good times and bad
Of merry go rounds and
Relationships we've had.

We've laughed til it hurt
And shed some tears
And loved each other
Throughout the years.

We'll be a team of four
Forever and a day
Not even death's sting
Can take that away.

Love you guys!

A Veteran's Salute

Here's a salute to those who served
On land, at sea and in air
We are so very thankful
For all of you being there.

Some gave their lives so gallantly
Some survived with wounded hearts
They hold their heads up high
While in life they still embark.

We owe so much to those who gave
Their duty they served for me
So that all of mankind
Could live a life that's free.

So when you're given that red poppy
Wear it on your lapel with pride
Just remember it's a symbol
For those who fought and died.

<u>Only So Much</u>

There's only so much that I can do
To cheer you up when you are blue
To pick you up when you are down
To show you that I'm always around.

There's only so much time in a day
To turn your clouds from a misty gray
To put a smile upon your face
To help you see God's loving grace.

There's only so much life to live
To be a giver and forgive
To add some joy to someone's day
To spread some cheer along the way.

So make the most of each new day
'Cause life's end is just a breath away
Remember today is tomorrow's memory
And yesterday is a moment in time for thee.

This poem started out directed to someone very close to me. But I realized it applies to anyone I come in contact with.
There are so many people that need an encouraging word and I hope this helps.

Magestic Moments

Majestic monuments formed by God
Now covered by the snow
Standing tall against all odds
While facing winter's blow.

The snow covered winter greens
Linger in the evening's sun
Taking shapes of tall figurines
Showing nature's fun.

The creatures seem to appalled
While in their spot they stay
Waiting for this white blanket
To finally go away.

But when the snow has begun to melt
And the greens resume their place
They'll show the gratitude they felt
And smile upon God's face.

<u>Angel On The Hilltop</u>

While walking down a country road
A stranger I did see
Perched upon a grassy hilltop
Directly in front of me.

The closer I became to him
The clearer he did seem
His clothes were tattered and worn
But around him was a gleam.

As I approached, I ask of him
Where are you going today?
He said to me in a gentle voice
I happen to be going your way.

Now what a strange coincidence
A stranger I would meet
Who knew my path of travel
And there to me he'd greet.

We traveled to my destination
And as I turned to say goodbye
The stranger that walked beside me
Was nowhere nearby.

The thought of an angel
Became so perfectly clear
He was there to walk with me
While safely be so near.

You see we all have angels
Watching over us every day
To lead, guide and protect
And keep us out of harm's way.

Christmas Time Is Here

Christmas time is here
Time for laughter and cheer
Time to share some tales of old
Time to bring everyone into the fold.

It's a time of celebration
For God's joyous creation
This Holy night was Heaven sent
To honor the One for whom it's meant.

Time for little ones eager to unwrap
Their gifts and toys in a snap
Time for remembering those gone above
Time to be thankful - Tis the season for love.

© 11/20/2019, Alinda C Daniels

<u>Only One Life</u>

I've only one life on earth
To be what I must be
I'll be like a lighthouse
For everyone to see.

I must stand strong
And not stumble or fall
I must shine my light
To be seen by all.

I must be a witness
To tell of God's plan
To share His truth and love
Throughout all the land.

And when my life on earth has passed
I pray that I withstood the test
And been a beacon to everyone
To show I've done my very best.

Epitaph Of A Poem

The darkness falls around me
As I lie here in my bed
Thoughts are running oh so rapid
Filling up my head.

Words dying to be written down
On paper with a pen
Perhaps a new poem
Is about to begin.

Suddenly the mood has changed
No words ever written
It's 5 am and sleep is calling
This writer has been smitten.

A Children's Prayer

There's a children's prayer
When they lay down to sleep
A prayer that they ask
The Lord their soul to keep.

So simple is that little prayer
To remember on their quest
For the Father up above
To grant their last request.

If only we could keep in mind
This little child-like prayer
So happy would the Father be
When we could go up there.

So listen to the children
Before it gets too late
Say this prayer of earnest plea
Your soul...the Lord will take.

Heaven's My Reward

I may not be wealthy or rich
But I will reap my reward
When I cross through that golden gate
To be given that which is stored.

You see, I am far richer
Than earth's richest man
I have royalty in my veins
And a mansion in Beulah land.

My father is the King
Of a wonderful, everlasting place
And some sweet day
He'll greet me face to face.

Oh what a glorious day that will be
When all my joys I will share
With all my friends and loved ones
Who are gathered over there.

<u>Thanksgiving 1982</u>

It was Thanksgiving 1982
And the family was at home
Everyone gathered around the feast
Just waiting to get some.

But first grace needed to be said
As we looked around to see
Who would say a simple prayer
To let this moment be.

It had always been my daddy
But now he had passed on
This Thanksgiving is most difficult
Since daddy was now gone.

Well, momma stepped up to say
The traditional family grace
The mood was that of lingering tears
Around our little place.

But momma was a trooper
And I learned that she was strong
I'm so thankful for her guidance
And I know I can't go wrong.

Sweet Sweet Music

Oh, it's sweet, sweet music to my ear
When all the choir stands to cheer
What a glorious feeling I have inside
Longing with my Jesus to reside.

Oh, it's sweet, sweet music to my soul
Just feeling His touch as thunder clouds roll
And takes me to that beautiful land
Where I will join the angels hand in hand.

Oh, it's sweet, sweet music to my heart
Where I know from Him I'll never depart
He is with me all day and night
From night's darkest hour until morning light.

Oh, it's sweet, sweet music I feel all over
Makes me want to roll in clover
Feeling the softness of God's tender touch
And knowing that He loves me so much.

Oh, this sweet, sweet music will last forever
All through life's trending endeavors
Just keep an open mind and listening ear
And you'll always hear it very near.

The Tears I've Cried

You know, Father, the tears I've cried
The endless nights I've laid awake
But you have kept these deep inside
Never with me did you forsake.

You've counted ever tear I shed
Recorded every pain I bare
Given me a ray of hope instead
And showed me that you really care.

If not for your love where would I be
Alone in sorrows I would dwell
But you alone doth comfort me
When hard times my life compels.

So forever be my keeper of life
My guardian and my friend
Keep me safe from toil and strife
And dangers may I apprehend.

When God Answers Prayers

When God Answers Prayers
You can feel a burden lift
When He answers your request
You can get the utmost gift.

He'll answer when you're lonely
Or when you're feeling down
He'll answer you wherever you are
He's there beside you, he's always around.

He'll answer when you're in pain
And you need to let out a cry
He'll hear you when you call for Him
He's always very nearby.

He'll answer when your heart is broken
Because of losing someone dear
He'll hold you in His loving arms
And dry away your tears.

Oh yes, when God answers prayers
Miracles do take place
Just take Him at His word
And lean upon His grace.

The Power Of The Cross

One cannot mistake the power of the cross
It's still standing when all is at a loss
It seems to appear daily in the sky
Or stands freely on a hilltop so high.

You can see it on the roadside
Where someone lost their life
And you can't help but wonder
Did it involve a sister, mother or wife?

You can see it still standing
After a terrible, stormy night
When the wind blows against it
It's still standing straight and upright.

You can see it on a battleground
Where a soldier fell in place
One who was protected
By God's mercy and His grace.

You can see it around someone's neck
Which symbolizes one's faith and love
Thank God for that rugged cross
Thank God for our home above.

Greater Is He

When I was young I never fully understood
The verse "Greater is He that is in you,
Than he who is in the world."
But as I've grown older, I've learned
This simple little Bible verse
Has more meaning than when a little girl.

The more I experience years in my life
The more I feel His love and power
And more I feel His wonderful grace.
He constantly reassures me
That He will always be around
To protect me in this earthly place.

As long as I have Him in my life
And I am faced with sudden fears
He will protect me in all situations.
He will cover me safety from all harms
And grant me a heavenly home
Just as He promises all believing generations.

Yes, I can feel His anointing power
And I am truly blessed each day
To have Him watching over me.
Instead of being in fear of things
I can thank the Lord above for blessings
Of peace of mind and a heart that is free.

You are of God, little children, and have overcome them, because He who is in you is greater than he who is in the world. I John 4:4

© 05/12/2021, Alinda C Daniels

<u>Faith</u>

FAITH - a five letter word
An armor one should bare
It will guard you against the evil one
It will lift you up to the One who cares.

It can move a mighty mountain
And quench a river's thirst
It will answer your needed questions
Just seek the Master first.

When you are at your lowest
And you feel no place to turn
Just put your faith in Jesus Christ
And feel the strength return.

It will protect you in all dangers
Or guard you from all fears
Just stop and pray for faith
And feel the Almighty's hands appear.

Faith will unlock a lot of doors
It will fulfill a lot of dreams
Christ is always here to turn to
He's always around it seems.

But without faith it is impossible to please him: for he that cometh to
God must believe that he is, and that he is a rewarder of them that
diligently seek him.
Hebrews 11:6 KJV

The Puzzle

I watched her try to connect
The puzzle pieces together
It was as though I fit right in
But my feelings I couldn't gather.

I thought about the pieces
And how my life seemed so abrupt
Trying to fit my life together
Caused my tears to erupt.

I thought about my childhood years
And the struggle to fit in
I remembered all the times
I just didn't seem to find joy within.

Then as I got older in life
I knew I was missing a piece
I felt I couldn't make the connection
Which would grant me eternal peace.

That's when I found the Savior
Knocking at my heart's door
Then all the pieces fit together
And I was in his presence forevermore.

© 17 hours ago, Alinda C Daniels

Holy, Holy Holy

Holy, Holy, Holy I will sing a song of joy
Almighty God, your creation to me amaze
Without your divine intervention
We would never exhalt your praise.

You are Holy and there's no one above you
You are the Father, the Son and the Holy Ghost
You created this world in seven days
A feat of which man cannot boast.

Father God Almighty, you created life
Into my lungs you gave me your humble breath
And when You determine my end has come
You will close mine eyes unto death.

Holy God and Father gently carry me
Lead and guide with loving hands
Praise be to the One whose name is Holy
And within the heaven's take thy stand

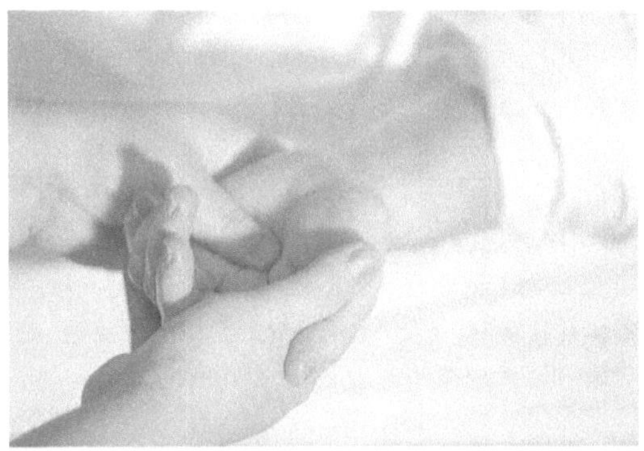

Feel My Hands

Put your hands in the loving hands of Jesus
Feel the nail scars left behind
Just know that when I died that day
I had you on my mind.

Imagine on that terrible day
As I hung upon the cross
In a most agonizing pain
I counted it all but a loss.

You see, I gave my life for you my child
So we could meet again
Just accept me as your Savior
Don't go down the path of sin.

Forever we can be together
In Heaven bright and fair
I'm looking forward some sweet day
To welcome you home with Me there.

<u>Miracles</u>

Miracles never cease to amaze me
As I'm faced with them each day
If it wasn't for the good Lord above
I'd never see them come my way.

I've often read of miracles in the Bible
That always caught my eyes
Like the virgin birth of Jesus
And Lazarus when he died.

But don't forget Sarah
Who was too old to give birth
The Lord saw to her needs
And fulfilled this woman's worth.

And as the crowds followed him
And the miracles took place
He healed the sick, the lame, the blind
It was glory, it was by His grace.

And when thousands of people gathered
To listen as the Master teaches
He fed them all until they were full
With only seven loaves and a few small fishes.

It was as though by each step He took
Someone needed His healing powers
Even today we seek Him through prayers
And He still blesses us at all hours.